What her critics are saying...

"I don't mean to gossip, but I have tried both their spaghetti methods, and his *is* better."
— *Mary Williams, social columnist*
Charlotte/AM Sarasota Herald-Tribune

"Our sympathies to the groom. Now he'll know what we've been going through all these years."
— *The Children*

"That's not a rummage sale, that's her desk."
— *Man in My Life*

"Sorry. There is no such thing as a yogurt and peanut butter cookie diet."
— *Doctor*

"Please stop writing about frogs in your toilet."
— *Tourism Official*

"The last thing you need is more pets."
— *Mother*

Linda Grotke Salisbury's first book

Good-bye Tomato, Hello Florida

Reviewers said ...

"Each page is amply laced with humor most writers only aspire to."

— *The Citizen, Auburn, N.Y.*

"A former Northerner, she writes about adjustment to Southwest Florida living and the struggle to forge at least civil relationships with domestic pets and a resident teen-ager.

"In the process, she does a literary high-wire act, managing to walk with skill and fun the tricky tightrope between burlesque and reality."

— *Fort Myers News-Press*

". . . a female Robert Benchley. . . . The author is forever baffled by life but copes by unnatural good nature. She has yet to win out over Florida's blandishments, her teenagers, her dog and cat, and household appliances. Nevertheless, her steadfast pursuit is guaranteed to make you laugh at least thrice per page."

— *Charlotte Herald-News*

"A funny book about Florida living from a Yankee come south. Linda Grotke, columnist and writer for the *Sarasota Herald-Tribune* has written a clever book. . . . the laughs come . . . often. A must read!"

— *The Review Committee*
National Association of
Independent Publishers

"She writes with an illuminating humor reminiscent of Erma Bombeck."

— *Sarasota Herald-Tribune*

What readers are saying...

"I enjoyed every page in your book. So many things hit home. When are you writing another?"

— *Jean Ganci*
West Palm Beach, Florida

"Your book is great! It's OUR FAMILY. All five of our kids will be ordered to read it. It put me on such a high that I've cancelled the next five sessions with my psychiatrist so you can see I can well afford to buy my own copy of *Tomato* and return the one I filched from my sister-in-law."

— *Yours for a Laugh-in World*
South Harwich, Massachusetts

"(The) book arrived Friday, and I spent Friday and Saturday evenings giggling and guffawing."

— *Ellen Price*
New York City

"Imagine our double delight when we checked into the Malabar House Bed and Breakfast in Union Springs, N.Y., and found *Goodbye Tomato, Hello Florida* in our room. We were familiar with it from our library at home. What a funny lady—we can't wait to read her new book."

— *Ralph and Mary Rubinstein*
North Reading, Massachusetts

"...I have never laughed so hard. The part about grits just cracked me up! (I hate grits!!) Everytime I put the book down, my husband picks it up..."

— *Tallahassee, Florida*

Read My Lips: No New Pets!

LINDA GROTKE SALISBURY

TABBY HOUSE BOOKS

Manufactured in the United States of America

Library of Congress Catalog Card Number: 90-71430

ISBN: 0-9627974-0-5

TABBY HOUSE BOOKS
4429 Shady Lane, Charlotte Harbor, FL 33980

For Man in My Life

Kith and Kin

with thanks to God for
His gifts of love

Acknowledgements

Because the stories which appear in my columns and books are drawn from actual happenings, similarities to living persons are hardly coincidental. Special thanks to my husband Jim, and children Chris, Abbie and Jen for their inspiration, tolerance and encouragement. And to Chester Baum for his editing; son Chris (an animator at the Capital Children's Museum) for his delightful artwork; David Kowal, Lorraine Toner and Judy Heekin for design ideas; Mary Williams, Jean Martensen, Lauren Patterson and Nancy Miller for assistance with some of the important details; and the steadfast support of many, many friends, family, *Sarasota Herald-Tribune* editors and readers.

Introduction

Linda Grotke Salisbury is a very funny lady. And she has the gift of translating her comedic view of life into engaging prose.

That's no small talent. Most writers I know shy from comedy, because it is a high-wire balancing act. It's much harder than it looks. And if you fall — if your stuff isn't funny — the whole world seems to know.

Imagine amusing your readers every week. Even harder. For seven years. Harder still. But that's what Linda has done, making her fans — and I'm one of them — smile, chuckle and laugh out loud at the 600 words or so she contributes every Wednesday to the *Sarasota Herald-Tribune*.

Linda's columns are not what you might expect to find in the opinion pages of a larger newspaper. And that's the charm. She writes about the real world, and she draws us into seeing things her way.

Her topics range from the ridiculous to the sublime. She writes about dogs, dentistry, diets, gardening, raising teens, raising kittens, fashion, getting lost at the mall, spring cleaning, vegetables, life in Florida, and whatever else comes to mind.

And she has a quirky way of finding the wry humor, and the laughter, in all she surveys. From the Salisbury shorthand (readers know her Man in My Life and Youngest Child as familiar figures) to her deadpan one-liners, she's an original. What higher praise is there in this age of packaged everything?

Her writing reflects her full, rich life. She's a mother, wife, former newspaper reporter, gardener, businessperson, musician, and friend to many. After you read her essays, you wouldn't be surprised to discover that in real life she is warm, gracious, intelligent, and, very funny.

So be prepared to be charmed, and amused. Welcome to the club of Mature Adults (and others) who enjoy Linda Salisbury's delightful musings.

Jefferson Flanders
Publisher
Charlotte/AM Sarasota Herald-Tribune

CONTENTS

His Pans, Her Clocks, Their Pets

He wants us to use *his* pots and pans. And he wants me to set all my clocks on the same time. He likes his sofa better.

We are in the middle of earnest prenuptial negotiations which are more difficult than I had realized for two middle-aged persons working out the details of combining households.

I figured that once we had convinced our elderly pets of the joys of adjusting to each other, the worst would be over.

The self-help books disregard our situation. While there has been a lot written about blended families, our children are grown and out of the nest. So we do not qualify as a prototype for a new sitcom series next fall on combining large numbers of precocious kids under one roof.

No bridal magazine I have read to date has provided advice on how to keep His Dog and Her Dog from fighting over a squeaky pork chop toy or who is most deserving of the cat's affections. Nor do they provide advice on whether old pets can be replaced some day by new ones.

Nor have they talked about the clock debate. And this issue is even more critical because of the impending time change.

It started when Man in My Life asked me a trick question the other night. He said, "What time is it?"

I said, "I don't know — look at the clock."

He said, "Which one?"

How could I be so blind? All these months he never confessed before how much it bothered him that none of the clocks in my house show the same time as any other. Some are fast, some are slow, and some might be right.

One clock, in a guest bedroom, doesn't show time at all. It blinks 12:00 because it is digital and needs resetting by someone who knows how. I don't.

Having matching timepieces, with all hands in perfect synchrony obviously doesn't matter to me. I never noticed the difference, or cared enough to do anything about it.

But for MML, who matches his socks when they come out of the dryer, my ability to live in an imprecise time zone of my own is disconcerting. But hey, I'm a Mature Adult. I'm glad he is expressing himself rather than picking a wrong clock to live by and maybe getting to our wedding late.

Another friend (he will sit on the groom's side of the church) said he also is concerned about knowing the exact time. He regularly calls Boulder, Colorado, to set his watch. That's where the Bureau of Standards is located.

His wife (who will be seated on the bride's side) whispered to me that a 10-minute differential from kitchen to bedroom clocks is fine with her too.

I have never given mismatched clocks much thought. When I reset all of them due to time changes or power failure, I go by the battery clock in the kitchen, which I set ahead so I get places on time. How much ahead, I'm not quite sure. Then I try to remember the kitchen time as I get to the other clocks in the house.

They only approximate the fast kitchen clock, according to how distracted I am in my wanderings through the house. I figure in the long run, it all evens out, much as does my unbalanced checkbook.

Confidentially, that is another matter I would rather you didn't discuss with MML, who balances his to the penny each month. I've been trying to find out a way to break it to him gently that I don't bother to open my statements. He's mature. He can handle it.

But the pans. I had no idea MML was so attached to his pans.

I had no idea I was so attached to mine.

Friends asked him if his were a better set. He said it didn't matter. His pans feel right in his hands.

Flexibility and compromise are obviously going to be the key to making our marriage work.

He can have socks that match, as long as I don't have to worry about mine and can borrow his.

He can use his pans as long as I can pick toothbrush colors (we've both always used blue).

We are grown-up. We can be rational without litigation about whose sofa goes in the living room.

Or maybe I'll offer to negotiate mine and the right to set the clocks, for one sauce pan, the squeaky pork chop and my stereo, recliner chair, coasters and . . .

Adventures
of a Middle-Aged Bride

The Dog Boys are exhausted after two weeks of heavy holiday begging. The groom is recovering from an auto accident and the flu. The Bride doesn't know where anything is in the house, thanks to the children.

It is middle-age marriage, American-style. And we have survived.

However, I was beginning to wonder about Man in My Life — whether he was trying to tell me something subconsciously.

First, a woman ran a stop sign, causing an accident which nearly totaled his car and injured his thank-you-note-writing arm.

Then, he was called for jury duty the week of the wedding.

Finally, he came down with the flu, just hours after the cake was cut.

His new bride, remembering her vows to love in sickness and in health, immediately rallied to the occasion. She took this opportunity to show MML that as a mother of grown children, she knows how to make chicken soup, read a thermometer and provide appropriate comfort.

She has also forgiven the supervisor of elections and county clerk for their invitation for MML to be selected for the jury during this important week of her life. She is mindful that MML always wanted to be on a jury, and in his entire adult life never had been called.

The Bride sweetly told him he had every right to choose between her and his duties to the judicial system. She said it even might help if he were sequestered under the circumstances, should he select the courthouse over the church. He wisely asked for a rain check for the jury pool.

The Bride was surprised to discover in the prenuptial process that she was more likely to be taken as the prospective "mother of . . ." than as The Bride herself. She learned the hard way that once a female gets beyond the "blushing" phase of life, she is not readily identified for her central role at the altar.

She went shopping at the mall for suitable low-heeled shoes to wear down the aisle — shoes which an ungraceful person could manage. Shoes comfortable enough to stand in during the reception.

She picked a pair from the store wall display when the young clerk approached her.

"And what is the occasion?" he asked.

"A wedding," she answered.

"Hmmm. And what color will you be wearing?"

"White," she answered, assuming that would identify her properly.

Obviously not.

"Could I show you a matching handbag to carry?" asked he, helpfully.

"The bridal bouquet will be sufficient," said she.

It was a good thing her daughters weren't along. The entire bridal party might have been carrying their flowers in matching purses.

And a word about having "adult" children involved with the wedding. This bride, who is now available for consultations to other middle-aged brides-to-be, would advise seeking effective means of controlling such offspring at this most serious of occasions.

The Bride's rule is this: Tie their behavior to your will.

Tell them they will receive any and all leftovers in next year's Christmas stocking.

Tell them you will pick out all their future clothing instead of sending gift certificates.

Then try to guess what they are planning and stay one step ahead.

It didn't work. MML and The Bride were suspicious when their combined offspring and visiting cousins seemed thoroughly uninterested in their post-reception departure for the night, throwing no rice and asking no questions.

So the new couple made new evasive plans, and left clever poems at strategic locations to let the children know they had been outfoxed should they have any pranks planned.

However, they should have known better. The welcome-home note on the front door read: "You forgot the most obvious! How could you leave us alone? Ha! Ha! We figured you wouldn't be going where you said you'd go . . . Love, the children."

Apparently the children had become immediately active as the newlyweds drove off — rearranging every piece of furniture in the house and hanging every picture upside down.

Figuring she would be blamed as usual, Youngest Child, 18, left a note of her own saying, "I didn't do it."

Bride's rule No. 5: If a middle-aged couple wants to avoid instant redecoration of their house, take the adult children with them on their honeymoon, or hire a competent sitter, who will read the provisions of the will as needed during the course of the evening.

As for the Dog Boys, The Bride says until they lose five pounds each, they are to be ignored in their embarrassing begging. Unfortunately, along with the happy couple, the dogs have become accustomed to living on Easy Treat during all the festivities.

Among other vows at the start of the New Year, The Bride "pledges her trough" will be less caloric.

Read My Lips: No New Pets

While we were waiting for several weeks for permission to complete our pool, after a zoning snag stopped work, a young boy who visits our house looked at the great earthen hole and said, "If you catch any neat animals in it, can I have them?"

The pool-hole looked like a trap to me, too — large enough to catch a rhino or bear.

I remembered my fascination with traps when I was eight or so. I was especially impressed with ones that Indians made and I daydreamed in class about digging large holes in our suburban back yard and catching something exciting.

It was so simple, according to my books. All you needed was a large hole and something to cover it, like branches or trees. Maybe some bait.

And then it was just a matter of sitting behind a bush and waiting for something big to come crashing along and fall in. You hoped it wouldn't be your mother. It would be easier to deal with an enraged bear.

Holes that size, for trapping wild beasts, were not approved under the deed restrictions in my Long Island neighborhood, so I never had a chance to try out my Indian lore.

Behind our pool excavation site is a large jungly woods, so I can see why young Mark was so interested in the hole's potential as a trap. There was plenty of palmetto to place over the top and some piles of dirt to hide behind while waiting for the wild beast to misstep and become ours.

But we didn't get at the trapping project soon enough. The zoning snag was solved and pool construction resumed.

However, the remodeling debris has become home to some unexpected "wildlife."

No sooner had my new husband said, "Read my lips: No new pets," than the pool workers discovered The Kittens.

They did not belong to Fluffy, our cat, and, to tell you the truth, she is none too pleased to have another feline living in her territory.

Mother Cat, a stranger to us, decided that an upside-down cast iron bathtub was just the right place for a birthing room and kitten nursery.

When Man in My Life signaled me over to see what had been discovered, I thought he wanted to show me a snake. Men are like that sometimes. Fortunately for both of us, it was kittens. And he is the first one out to feed them in the morning, despite his pet edict.

The second time the pool workers made an animal discovery, it *was* a snake, and not a friendly variety at that. They took it away in a plastic water jug to show their friends. Men are like that sometimes.

My mother was not an animal lover. She barely tolerated the family dog who lived to old age out of spite. I was not allowed to have a kitten, and therefore a cat was totally out of the question.

Her standard explanation for turning down my infrequent request was "kittens grow up to be cats." That was that. No arguing with her.

So these little balls of grey fur are a delight. I want them to love me. They don't. They love their own mother. They scream when I pick them up. I am suffering from kitten rejection.

I want them to lick my fingers and purr. They don't. They holler and yowl and want to go back where it is dark, in their cave home.

MML, who has had many cats in his life, says The Kittens act that way because they are just a few days old.

8

I want to buy them catnip and balls of yarn to play with. MML says that I should wait until they open their eyes and can walk. He says I should not give catnip to minor kittens just to get them to come out. He says it is against the law. "Just say no," he counsels The Kittens.

But I don't want to wait until they are *old* kittens. I want to play with them now.

Fluffy was not a kitten when Middle Child selected her on one of our trips to the animal shelter to adopt a pet.

Cat and child had an instant bond. Fluffy slept with her, sat on her lap and waited by the front door when Abbie went off for college.

She was still waiting by the front door five years later even though she was no longer sure which door Abbie would come back through.

Then one night recently, in a fit of disloyalty to Middle Child (who has since acquired kittens up north), Fluffy jumped in my lap.

"Do you know, in 15 years, Fluffy has never sat in my lap?" I said incredulously to MML, who was watching the evening financial report on television.

"Cats do that," he said.

"I mean, why now? I don't know if I should feel honored," I said.

"Pet her," said MML engrossed in the news.

"Do you know, in 15 years I have never really petted Fluffy? I never really thought about it before. I mean, she's sat in your lap and you've petted her, but I never cared that she ignored me. And here she is in my lap, kneading me with her claws. Ouch."

"Cats are like that," he said.

I suppose it takes awhile to get to know a cat. We don't know if Mother Cat will stay once her children are grown. Or if suddenly someday she will parade them past our concrete bear trap back into the woods, with hardly a backward meow.

As a precaution, I'd better read up on how to build a kitten trap. I think I remember that the Indians used a cardboard carton, a stick with a string tied to it and a catnip mouse dangled as bait.

House of Fun

It was enough to send maternal chills down my spine.

It was the moment of truth that mothers never expect, especially from the "good child."

She was the one who always came home on time during high school. Like me.

She was the one who always could be located where she said she would be during the evening.

She could be counted on to feed the cats and take care of her dolls. Like me.

She even practiced her French horn without a reminder from her mother.

So you can see why I am in shock.

We, this exemplary 21-year-old person and I, had just concluded a lovely phone conversation late Saturday afternoon, when I remembered I had forgotten to ask her something important.

I called New Bedford again. There was no question it was my daughter's voice.

"Abbie's House of Fun, how may I help you," she said.

"AAABBBBBIIIEEE, this is your MOTHER. . . ."

Now I always believed that a home should provide an environment of fun, and ours was no exception. In fact, given the imagination, irrepressible humor and high spirits of my three children, we needed little out-of-home entertainment during their formative years.

But House of Fun?

Is this what they teach in college?

I should have wondered if I would have problems later in life with her when she was in high school band. She was the only student who had not been in trouble. She was always prepared, had her horn polished and her music memorized. She was dependable. Like me.

But one cold rainy night, when a small, volunteer pep band sat in the drizzle at an away game at which her team was losing, Abbie got in trouble. Big trouble with the director.

She came home in tears, having been thoroughly chastised on the bus ride back in front of all the other students.

"What's the matter?" I asked, expecting my shy, well-behaved child to confess to purloining the contents of the entire concession stand or to painting "don't you wish, you could be a fish," where Tarpon supporters were sitting in the stands.

Through her sobs, the story came out. A trumpet player had begged her to teach him how to play "nana nana boo boo" on his instrument.

Bored and sitting in the rain, she did — and got caught.

Yes, it must have started that night, because she had never before shown any signs of this sort of behavior.

She brushed her teeth. She didn't read other people's diaries. She drove within the speed limit during her driver's test. She never laughed at the wrong time in church. Like me.

Maybe it is just a passing phase, caused by the stress of winter in the north, college exams and a new cat. She had a rigorous adoption proceeding last week at the animal shelter. She was interviewed over a two-day period as to suitability as a pet owner.

She went back with pictures of Fluffy and the dog, and came home with calico Mabel.

Maybe that is it. Maybe she was just wanting to invite her friends over to have fun at her house with her new cat. They will roll yarn balls around and watch Mabel pounce. And then they will all have some milk and cookies, take turns holding her and listening to her purr.

So I don't need to worry any more.

Nana nana boo boo.

Bridal Defense Committee — A Sticky Situation

Humpff.

The middle-aged bride (mother of three), has had her first "failure" in the kitchen since the December wedding.

It boils down to this. Man in My Life does not like my technique for cooking spaghetti. He says the long thin strands of pasta should not, he repeats, should not be broken in half and put in lukewarm water to cook.

And furthermore, my culinary critic continues, I should stir it with something other than a shish kabob skewer.

Humpff.

He suggests that I read directions. Then, he says, he also might not find something that looks like transatlantic phone cable buried in his sauce.

Humpff.

Does he care to hear from the Bridal Defense Committee?

I have good reasons for all but the pasta cable.

Spaghetti is long and thin. No one, including the Italians, makes the right shape cooking container for it. I break mine to fit in the round pan, so I don't have to stand there when I have other things to do, waiting for it to soften, then bend into the water.

Because I have other things to do, I also don't like to wait around for the water to boil. An alternate method is to let it heat up, and get some other work done in the house. Unfortunately when I return, I find only a small amount left which has not become steam.

And thirdly, the skewer was handy. Most of my kitchen utensils are packed in preparation for the move to the new house.

Humpff.

"I'm a failure in the kitchen," I told Middle Child, expecting her to rally to my defense.

"What did you cook?" she asked carefully.

"Spaghetti. The sauce was wonderful — full of things you didn't like as a child — onions, mushrooms, peppers."

She asked carefully, "Were the noodles all glumped together?"

Humpff.

Unfortunately, time has not taken away her memory. Erase her name from the Mother Defense Committee!

On at least one occasion, the glumpy noodles were not caused by their incubation in lukewarm water, slowly rising to a boil.

A guest, a friend of Middle Child, had been substantially late for dinner.

Because the "honored guest" was normally prompt, the mother did what a good mother would do. She went ahead and started the pasta so the food would be ready the moment the guest appeared.

Unfortunately, we learned spaghetti changes its consistency in 45 minutes of boiling.

The children said they preferred bowls of sauce — hold the glump, please.

The Bridal Defense Committee says that newlyweds have many important things on their minds, and need to learn many things.

The BDC says that sometimes a young, first-time bride may read how to prepare each dish of the meal, and do so correctly, but fail to time them so they are all completed simultaneously.

My first meal for company many, many years ago involved rice, frozen peas, some sort of affordable meat, a stove the size of a place mat, no countertop and two pans.

I followed the directions for each ingredient of the meal, starting all at the same time. The peas were done instantly, the meat a few minutes later, and the rice after dessert. It was what is commonly called a learning experience.

The middle-aged bride may have the timing down, but needs either to persuade the man in her life that broken spaghetti is the trendy way to prepare it, or undo all her bad habits in the kitchen.

Since the first option is out, I'm stuck with "mending my ways," or letting someone else do the cooking.

The BDC (with a membership of one), having failed to convince her husband that broken spaghetti is preferable and having received thumbs down from mutual friends and children as well, will stick to sauce rather than learn how to boil water at this late date. MML says he will do both, thank you.

Hmmmmm. I think I'm on to something.

13

Retting Out a Lifetime's *Cultch*

Maine'rs have the word for it: *cultch*.

While I'm not exactly sure of the spelling, *cultch* is how it sounds. And it means all that special, quality clutter, of which I have a lot.

I presume this lovely addition to my vocabulary takes its derivation from the word "culture." If not, I would like to hear from those of you who know and can set me straight on this and other words I intend to sprinkle liberally among my usual language.

I like the word *cultch*. It gives the clutter I treasure a new shine. And, as I understand it, if I am sorting through and getting rid of some of it (no doubt at great price to some antique or collectible shop) I would be *retting out* my *cultch*.

Most of my spare time this weekend has been spent in retting out. It was in anticipation of great crowds of relatives during the holidays. I retted out quite a bit of it in boxes for my children, and took them to a parcel service to be sent north. The man asked me to describe the contents of each. I had no idea. It had been hours and hours of retting out and packing, and sneezing. I could not remember the last time anyone had dusted in our limited storage areas.

"Cultch," I said.

"Could you be more specific," he asked, pen poised.

"Frankly, no. I've been cleaning out the children's closets all day, and I can't remember who got what. Can't you just put down 'stuff'?" I asked.

Evidently not. It is against parcel sending rules. They want to know the gory details of what I found during my archeological dig.

"Well," I said, rallying with my new vocabulary, "This box has something *gormey* with wheels in it."

He wrote down "toys," and tossed it on the pile of other cartons.

Gormey means (for those of you not taking Mainese lessons, as I am), something large and not handsome. Something overly done and in poor taste. I suspect my grandmother's cocoa set might fall into that category. Also a couch I had once. Perhaps even the dog.

I wonder if there might be some cultch which is also gormey, but that may be in my next lessons.

I always thought I was from The North until I met people who were from farther north. They have their own language, much as Southerners do. I want to be able to communicate with them and welcome them when they come for winter visits. It puts them at ease to say a little something indigenous when you are sitting next to a Vermont car at a long traffic light.

"Burlington, Ben & Jerry's ice cream, maple syrup, Green Mountain boys," I wave, and smile. They look so pleased at my effort to speak in their native tongue.

But, until I complete my course, that is as far as it goes for that little state. If they had asked me questions in reply, I would have been stumped.

I've discovered our town is a real melting pot. You can hear dialects from all over the map while you're shopping for soft drinks — and find out that some people next to you are buying "soda" and others, "pop," and some are seeking the same thing, but call it "tonic." It is wonderful to be so cosmopolitan.

And to tell the truth, I don't mind stopping by a Christmas tree stand and asking the vendors if they can speak a little Michiganese — maybe teach me a few expressions.

After years in this neck of the palmetto, I long for my native language — Middle North.

My children will be so happy to hear that I haven't lost my native accent that they will not be upset when carton after carton of cultch arrives in their tiny apartments.

I know it will be a strain on the storage space. Two years ago, my son barricaded his door to the postman. He said, "If it has a Florida return address, send it back!"

He said to the man in blue, "If it says, 'Fragile: Homemade Christmas cookies,' call the EPA."

He said, "If she sends me any more of my baby clothes, I'll get all the cats in my neighborhood and dress them."

I don't know why he doesn't want the stuff he wants me to save for him.

It is part of the rights of parents, written up, I think, in my Dr. Spock. Parents have the right to send cartons of cultch, gormey or not, after children reach maturity and have either a closet or floor space. That includes junior high yearbooks, college term papers, elementary school valentines, and instructional music (Book 1) for drums and guitars. Also the drum and guitar.

With a bit of luck, a friend will *kife* some of it — that is "casually steal" a bit — or my kids can do their own retting out in their free time.

The boxes are on their way. The cats of Washington will be well dressed for the holidays.

Miter Makes Right

They were so proud of their handiwork. In a very short amount of time they had removed half the tile from around the tub, sink and vanity and were headed down the homestretch with the rest of the fixtures.

Unfortunately, it was the wrong bathroom in our newly purchased house.

I was the one to break the news to the happy crew.

"I'm just stopping by to see if you guys are working on the right bathroom," I said.

"And . . . you're not. Let me show you the right one," I said.

"Oh no! Oh no!" said the demolition experts, banging their heads in dismay on every wall in sight.

"Oh yes," said I. "You simply didn't go far enough into the house. We weren't planning to remodel the guest bathroom at all."

"Oh no! Oh no!" said the crew, banging their fists on their foreheads.

I wasn't as upset as you might expect. Frankly, I didn't like the tile which they had inadvertently removed. It had a color pattern best described in decorating magazines in the mid-Seventies as flecks of mud on harvest gold globs. I hoped it was irreplaceable.

My sympathies immediately went out to these fellows — to see their labors in vain and unappreciated.

16

I know how difficult construction — or de-construction — projects can be. Back in the days when I tackled more of them myself, I wished I had made more than just one birdhouse in elementary school shop class.

Girls took home economics when I was in fourth grade, and were allowed to get the feel of a hammer and nails through a simple birdhouse project. We were not expected to need to know how to fix anything or make shelves.

Boys got to build grand things, learned to use screwdrivers and power tools and once a year made brownies as their preparation for adult life.

So I was ill prepared, after my divorce, to cope with major necessary home improvements in our older home, based on a two-week study of birdhouse construction many years earlier.

Lack of experience or knowledge did not daunt me, however. I said to Oldest Child, then 11, "We can do this together." He had an ample workbench in the cellar. I was counting on his expertise.

We had, in storage, a fine supply of paneling, which I figured would cover a myriad of problems associated with lack of adequate plaster.

We purchased 10 pounds of colored nails and struggled up the stairs with great sheets of paneling. The project was successful as long as we didn't have to cut the sections to fit the wall. We just leaned them up, taking turns pounding nail after nail into the finished plywood.

Over a period of time, we were sure to hit studs in the wall so that the paneling would be secure.

Suddenly, we were in crisis. The wall had an angle in it, and then another along the ceiling edge. My birdhouse had not been this complicated.

What to do. Lacking good spatial skills, I figured the best way to get the paneling to fit was to make a paper pattern. I found some large pieces of newsprint and creased it along the angles of the wall, brilliantly traced on the wood and cut.

It was pretty good. All I needed was something to fill the 4-inch gap between wood and ceiling.

Molding became my new best friend. Wide molding. Very wide. And I got myself a miter box and, for a brief moment of glory, which I never dared to repeat, I mitered.

It worked.

Heady with success, I wallpapered, and replaced electrical

17

outlets. I assembled ceiling fans from scratch, and let my son bake the brownies.

It didn't matter if the fan blades were upside down. What counted was that, when I turned the switch, the blades moved. Who says girls can't do electrical projects?

I wish I could tell you that I went on to a grand career of home remodeling — passing exams for courses at Vo-Tech without even attending class. I would like to report that my handiwork was admired by the people who bought my house Up North.

Maybe they just didn't like molding in so many unusual places, but as near as my former neighbors can figure, they gutted the interior and started over after the deal closed.

I would like to tell you that my helpful efforts are appreciated.

More-than-patient Man in My Life gives me cheery helpful hints on painting woodwork. His way takes longer. I can do mine twice in the time it takes him to do his. And he is making me do just that, to cover over little "holidays" in the paint — where areas were skipped. So I get to paint my sections twice.

I did wallpaper my study. It looks great as long as I am standing in a spot where I can block off the messy corner with an elevated left arm.

You see, something happened as I made a sudden right turn near a door. I'd rather not talk about it and I would just as soon you didn't ask.

But it is minor compared to the condition of the guest bathroom. And based on past experience, it's nothing a trip to the molding department won't take care of.

I wonder where I packed my miter box.

Oh no! Oh no!

Pets Heighten a
Moving Experience

The notation on the envelope said, "Returned for better address." That was an understatement from the friendly folks at the post office. The letter I had sent out had no address at all.

It was a part of a mass mailing, done single-handedly at work by yours truly. Then four more envelopes came back for postage. I remembered to address them, but forgot the stamps.

I might as well have hired the Dog Boys to do the job.

They are in a very helpful mood these days. They anticipate my every step and get there first.

If I want to wash a baseboard in preparation for painting, they know exactly which one and mark it with a heavy, sleeping body.

They cleverly guess which wall is freshly painted and sit next to it, close enough to absorb all the excess on their shoulders.

In short, we have learned that the Dog Boys, who were born with black fur, are attracted to anything that lightens their color.

The smaller dog looks most days like he works in a bakery. The powder with which he is dusted comes from sanded plaster. We sand, he rolls in it.

He managed to walk through a roller pan of white paint. Actually off-white. The roller pan was in a straight line between the smaller dog and his water dish. And, as we all learned in elementary school, the shortest distance between two points is a straight line.

Rascal, well-named as a puppy, waded all four paws through the pan and padded directly for the kitchen, leaving prints that made for easy tracking. No special detective work needed.

I discovered that cleaning paint out of four cocker spaniel paws is worse than getting oil-base paint out of a roller. In fact, my solution to the latter is to throw away the brush or roller if circumstances dictate the use of oil-base paint. I could not do the same with paws.

The Dog Boys have an uncanny ability to know which room we will be carrying boxes from, and they decide to sleep in the doorway. It is the same ability that lets them select the only part of the back yard that is muddy and wade through it, or the sandiest part to roll in.

Fluffy, the cat, has not coped well with the move. Basically, she has tried to ignore it. She did not offer to help paint or pack, but preferred to sun herself outside.

But once the furniture was out, she came skidding through the door and immediately took notice. In all the years Fluffy has lived with us, I have never seen her look quite so surprised.

The only other time her face could not have disguised a poker hand was when she made a dramatic bid for escape in Atlanta when we were moving to Florida in 1978. After two days in the car with three children and The Dog, Fluffy decided enough was enough and headed for the bushes at a motel.

I knew we would never be able to leave until the cat was safely back in Middle Child's custodial arms. And not wanting to spend the rest of my life in a motel parking lot, I led the safari through the prickly bushes. Fluffy was visible, suddenly deaf, suffering from amnesia, and three steps ahead of us.

It was quite a parade. Cat, mother, and three children.

"Fluffy, want a shrimp?" I asked.

"Fluffy, you can ride in the front seat," said Oldest Child.

"Fluffy, I'll get you a year's supply of catnip when we get to Florida," said Middle Child.

"Fluffy, you can sleep on mom's pillow," generously offered Youngest Child.

"That's going too far," I said. But Fluffy stopped. She pretended to be looking at a jaybird.

A deal was a deal. Oldest Child gave up his seat to the cat, Middle Child mortgaged her Barbie dolls, and I put Fluffy outside every night with my pillow.

This time around I borrowed a cat-carrying case and transported Fluffy in a no-risk move.

I don't want to make any more deals with the cat.

Signs of Order

I knew I was being watched as I rummaged in my purse for Chapstick. There was a sudden prolonged silence in the car.

"I'm not going to say anything," said the driver.

"Just because it takes awhile to find something doesn't mean that I don't need everything in there," I said, hoping I would find the plastic tube quickly.

"I'm not saying anything," replied the driver.

"Then watch the traffic and stop timing my Chapstick hunt," I said.

"Did you hear me say a word?" he asked.

Man in My Life and I were born under different signs. As a Gemini, I live under the sign of clutter. Its astrological logo is a decorative two-lidded trash can: one side to throw things in, and the other to take them back out of when you need them.

MML was born under the sign of the neat and orderly. His astrological logo is a goat which eats clutter. He throws away junk mail before it arrives. He cleans the kitchen before it gets messy. He keeps important papers in files and labels the files with exactly what is in them. He knows what is in his pantry.

I fantasize about what living that type of life might be like. I wonder what it would be like to wash my coffee pot on a regular basis.

After all these years I have identified my problem. It all has to do with my horoscope.

No matter what day I check this advice in the paper, it never said, "Your stars indicate that it would be an auspicious day to clean and sort," or "Weed your junk drawer today and you will have a pleasant evening ahead."

When I read newspapers, my astrological advice column never counsels me to empty my purse and throw stuff out.

I use my purse the way men use their pockets or a briefcase. Or both. Men are just more subtle about carrying important things with them. People expect briefcases to be heavy. They are constructed of heavy-looking material. So if they are filled with files or mini-tape recorders and pocket computers, cameras and lunch for four, in addition to files and legal pads, it's a surprise to no one.

My purse, which needs luggage wheels and a leash, shocks the unwary. I can't say it contains anything of value, except to me. *Stuff,* by definition, has value only to its owner. It's odds and ends. And things. It's the stuff which probably needs to be sorted and integrated into a house or office collection or pile, but for one reason or another isn't.

Stuff is more difficult to deal with than ordinary clutter, which at the most is shoved around or reorganized periodically from one room to the next.

It congeals between zippered pockets. It settles, gains weight and breeds as I drive around town, unable to find an isolated picnic table and trash can so I can dump everything out just to find my lip balm or a pen.

I could carry a briefcase and spread things out a bit. Then again, I could carry a suitcase and still not have everything I need with me at any given time.

So, when I purchase a purse, I try to keep its future weight in mind, but am somehow distracted by its versatility, as demonstrated by a clever sales clerk.

My rummaging is so far unsuccessful. However, I found other useful stuff — dog vitamins from his December trip to the vet. A bill I meant to mail. Some gum. A grocery list for a holiday party.

"Keep your eyes on the road and stop smirking," I said to the driver.

"I'm not saying anything," said he.

The Middle-Age
Wedding Folderol

My dentist says I can't walk down the aisle until I get a filling for a cavity in one of my teeth. My dentist says he has connections in the marriage license office.

He plays hard ball when it comes to getting his 10 most wanted patients back for their dental work, so I take his threats seriously, including reminders for return engagements.

However, the only engagement I am concerned with at the moment is my own. And I don't like the idea that before I can get on with my new life, I might have to bring a note from my dentist to the county courthouse.

It is giving new ammunition to Man in My Life's plea that we should just elope and skip all the folderol.

He is at one end of the spectrum of nuptial planning. Children and friends are at the other, and somewhere in the middle is the bride-to-be, who is avoiding her dentist.

Youngest Child says she has always wanted to plan a wedding. She is Up North at college, reading bridal magazines between classes.

"You've got to be traditional," she wails. She wants the full procession, possibly with the spotlight on the bridal attendants' entrance.

That will be fine. In fact, it may be the perfect distraction as the middle-aged bride and groom sneak in from the side door and take their place before the altar.

She is lobbying for new clothes for everyone.

"You know how I hate to shop," I say. "I've got a nice outfit I've only worn a couple of times . . ."

"You can't do that," she says from Central New York.

I suggest that while I will wear something I have, she and her sister should simply find something nice to wear, in holiday colors. But now that she has read the latest trends, she wants matching outfits.

"But you and your sister never liked the same type of clothes. You were the flashy, latest-fashion type, and you considered what

23

the rest of us wore dowdy. You mean you would like to wear the same thing as your sister?"

What she has in mind is that her sister would wear the same thing as she selects, and for once look like a woman of the Eighties or Nineties. Middle Child doesn't like miniskirts, so I'm not sure she will even go for a fitting.

"And what about the bouquets? What will mine be like?" says my young fashion consultant.

"I was thinking more of simple corsages," I respond.

"You've got to be traditional, Mom," she says. "And you can't throw a corsage to me."

"We can practice when you come home for Christmas," I suggest.

"Listen, Mom, you're never going to have another wedding."

She has a point. If I can get shy MML to meet me at the church in front of all those people to pledge his troth, it will be just this once. I know I cannot get him to do it a second time.

I ask my son if he will give me away.

A liberated male, he says, "I think that sounds rather chauvinistic. Can't we call it something else?"

"Do you like the sound of 'hand me over' better?"

He doesn't. And he wants his sisters to do whatever we decide to call it with him in unison.

A chorus of adult children; I suddenly don't trust them. I could never trust them in a group. It was for that reason I never dated as long as they were living at home. They were irrepressible.

How does a Mature Adult say good night to her date with three teens peeking out at the front curtain, then sending the youngest child out with a camera to see "what the noise is" in the driveway.

The groom-to-be has an adult daughter too. Can she be trusted or will she succumb to peer pressure? Or will she accept bribes from my dentist to put detour signs in front of the wedding procession so that suddenly we are in front of his office?

And so it goes. Man in My Life says he doesn't like to be the center of attention, where everyone will be looking at him. Frankly, I don't think he will have to worry about it. The spotlight will be on the bridesmaids in their matching outfits.

We will be so inconspicuous by contrast that I figure I'll need to wear a "Hello, My Name is The Bride" badge. At least, then, my dentist will recognize me.

Kittens on the Keys

I'm not sure if this constitutes grounds for an annulment, but I have learned that Man in My Life does not play the musical instrument that he implied he did during our courtship.

In one of our lengthy getting-to-know-you discussions, the subject of musical proficiency came up. In naming the instruments that I play or have tried to play or occasionally practice, I mentioned the recorder. He knew I didn't mean the electronic tape kind.

We were eating Chinese food and speaking of wooden flutelike things when MML allowed as to how he played one at some time in his life. I admit, in retrospect, he was a bit vague about when and for how long, but I tucked this musical skill away in my mind as something the two of us could do together on an evening when television was boring, or the Scrabble game was hidden beneath clutter.

Wrong. When others came over to play recorders, he disappeared from the sound of what he calls "kazoo" practice. And, when I pressed for a deeper explanation of his past experience, I learned that he had played the "sweet potato," or Flutaphone, in fifth grade. For six weeks. Everybody had to. He threw it in the bushes when the course was over.

And now he would rather watch almost anything on television than contemplate learning to read music and joining our little group.

My children will be delighted to know another family member has joined their numbers. One year, in the hopes of developing a family music group that might be as internationally-heralded as the Trapp family, I gave everyone a recorder for Christmas. This was before I met MML. Fortunately.

The novelty wore off as we struggled to play *Hark How the Bells* on Christmas Eve. The bushes were strewn with plastic sticks with holes in them on our way home from church.

I still say even badly played music is better than most television shows, especially when plots can be interchanged and you don't know it.

MML and I were watching television the other night. It was a movie about a little boy whose mother had left home and no one

25

was sure where she had gone. The plot centered on the boy's problems, with someone periodically asking where his mother was.

About halfway through the drama, MML and I took advantage of a commercial break for popcorn. When we returned, the action had shifted to a treatment clinic for women suffering from eating disorders.

"Is that the boy's mother?" I asked.

"Beats me," said MML.

We ate our popcorn.

"As part of her therapy, why don't they ask her why she abandoned her child?" I asked.

"Beats me," said MML.

We finished off the popcorn.

"You'd think they'd show the kid again or at least work him into conversation," I said.

"I think The Kittens changed the channel," said MML.

We both studied the television set. Sure enough. While we were in the kitchen, The Kittens walked on the remote control button and flipped us to another station.

"I won't tell if you won't," I said. "I feel a little silly, having spent 10 minutes trying to make sense of this strange twist in the plot."

"Don't tell," said MML.

Even The Kittens find somewhere else to play during recorder practice. They follow MML to his soundproof isolation booth, where he can listen to anything but our efforts at four-part Elizabethan rondos which we slow to our skill level. Very slow.

I could teach him how to play. We were all beginners once. He could catch up real fast if he just put in some quality practice time.

But, seeing that faraway look in his eye when I broach the subject, I suspect his attitude toward musical participation has not changed much since fifth grade. I doubt that MML will be playing *Hark How the Bells* as a part of a surprise holiday concert I am preparing for my children when they come home. Perhaps, now that they are more mature, they will want to try again.

More likely they and MML will be watching whatever program The Kittens select in another room.

Sergeant on the Brown Bag Beat

It has been a few years since I have served as Sergeant of School Lunches. As someone whose organizational ability cannot be measured by her desk, closets or bank statements, I should have been given a congressional medal for maternal brown sacking. Instead, I was defeated by bread sandwiches.

Two of my children preferred fasting to eating institutional food. They liked packing *anything* from home — because *anything* was better than cafeteria spaghetti with thick noodles. *Anything* was better than a goulash with kidney beans hidden in the sauce at the request of the health teacher.

For the picky eater, it meant less trauma to pack her brown bag. She knew who touched her sandwich and what it contained She had personally selected her snacks. Nothing was left to chance. There was no threat of dried beans, sunflower seeds, or other surprises.

Oldest Child was less finicky. But he preferred making his own lunch to allowing his mother to prepare darling little treats or pack clever embarrassing messages among his carrot sticks.

He threatened to leave home after St. Patrick's Day, second grade, when everything in his lunch box was green. After his doting mother had gone to all that trouble, her boy said, "Don't do that again."

He said his teacher took one look and called the health department.

To get children up and out for school is a task best left to a two-parent family — one to get them up, and the other to get them out.

So the single mother's strategy became: get the lunches made the night before. And the children were old enough to do it themselves. Thus the Sergeant of Lunches showed them a system for multiple-meal preparation. In a fit of amazing organization, each child might make a week's supply of sandwiches in a single evening and freeze them.

This accomplished two purposes. Everyone got out of the house in time for the school bell, and it was easier to fool The Dog.

The Dog went into daily mourning at the loss of his playmates. If he saw them making sandwiches or taking the brown bags to the car, his retribution in the house was doubled. Barbies were beheaded. Dirty underwear was strewn by the front door.

If the lunches were made in the evening, it was easier to sneak them out of the house the next morning. The Dog might think the family was off for a ride around the block, not gone for a long school day. Destruction was therefore minimized.

So my role as sergeant included making sure my young children had something in their brown sacks that was nutritious and wonderful, something worth coveting and trading at school.

Surely I would get the recognition from the PTA for my role, especially since my children were learning responsibility in the process. I trusted them to fulfill their lunch mission while I carried out my duties in the laundry room.

That was before I discovered the bread sandwiches.

They were the youngest child's efforts to save time away from the television. While I trusted her to apply liberal amounts of peanut butter and jelly to her bread — all she could eat — instead she took two slices from the bread bag, folded them neatly, and stuffed them in her brown sack.

Then, because of her ability to sweet talk anybody out of anything, she managed to trade her contributions to the school lunch program to some child who had come with a catered gourmet meal from home.

She hoarded milk money and played the stock market.

I was ruined.

It is probably in our family file at county schools. A brief notation from the cafeteria monitor: "Youngest Grotke eligible for cafeteria scholarship — uncaring mother sends her with bread sandwiches."

Since I never received my PTA award, my assumption is that this comment on our record has left me with a dishonorable discharge.

Betrayed by bread sandwiches, and without a hearing. I'm afraid to ask to have the case reopened. Someone official might ask about those St. Paddy's boiled eggs.

Better to Forgive, then Receive

It was a good thing the children came home one at a time at Thanksgiving. It would have been too much for The Dog's heart if they had all been on the same flight.

He has lived a quiet life in recent years. He can only dream of boys and girls scratching his back and feeding him treats of table scraps. He remembers an occasional game of ball and being forced to leave the room when, after eating cat food, he violated human olfactory propriety when the children had friends over.

But they have been gone for some time. In fact, he hadn't seen his boy in more than 18 dog years.

So when Middle Child arrived first, with a sack of fast food, The Dog was momentarily distracted by the fries. He didn't look up to see whose hand was holding the bag. Then, suddenly, his mental calendar flipped back 10 canine years to when she moved Up North. Yes, he did remember.

Good heavens, the one who loved Fluffy The Cat more had returned. But at least she had arrived with junk food in hand.

The Dog immediately forgave past excessive cat-loving for just one piece of cheeseburger (hold the onion, please).

Youngest Child missed her plane and came a day late. The Dog's heart had just settled down from Middle Child's arrival when the youngest came in the door eating cookies.

Who was she, The Dog asked? Oh, yes, the one who always threw him out of her room and stamped and screamed when he got into her Halloween candy. But for just one cookie, he'd forgive her immediately.

She had matured. She scratched his ears and said she had missed him. She no longer said he was ugly. She even said his face had character.

But The Dog had to be revived with smelling salts a few hours later when the 6-foot-4-inch boy arrived from Washington. No food. Just warm greetings for his graying pet.

A quick session with fur and paws and the oldest child said, "He's lumpy. Why is The Dog lumpy? He looks all lopsy."

"Gray. Our old friend was black and this dog is quite gray, and lumpy," said Middle Child.

"He's been into my cookies again," said Youngest Child. "Maybe the lumps are cookies."

"Old dogs just get lumpy sometimes," I said. "Look how he loves you. Look how he wants you to scratch where he can't reach. Wouldn't one of you like to inherit the dog, at a point when you could still enjoy him?" I asked.

There was silence in the living room.

"My landlord won't even let me take Fluffy," said the middle child.

"Washington is no place for an old lumpy dog," said my son.

"He'd steal too many cookies and probably do something gross while my boyfriend is around," said the youngest child.

"I thought you might like to play a game of Pet Lotto after our turkey dinner. I have some neat prizes. One for each of you," I said. "The Dog is first prize, unless the winner wants cats."

No takers. I was suddenly left with the dishes, some lumpy gravy and fear that The Dog would have child-departure retaliation syndrome. He would find some new and clever things to do with the laundry after I made three more trips to the airport, as his childhood friends headed north without him.

But it is almost Christmas. Pets make good presents. With a nice red bow and a plane ticket, the family Pet Lotto winner will be so surprised and pleased to hear that the grand prize is on his way, with a stocking full of flea dip and rawhide treats.

Summer Dieting; Summer Not

How many calories in computer paper? In my phone cord?

I'm getting desperate. It nears supper time of week number two on the Man in My Life's diet. His diet is mine as well.

MML's recent annual checkup included this dialogue:

Doctor: "I see you have been gaining some weight."

MML: "Mmmmmm."

Doctor: "About 15 pounds. What happened to the jogging?"

MML: "You see, I met this woman, and we've been eating out and . . ."

Doctor: "And she has gained 15 pounds too?"

MML: "Mmmmmm."

Doctor: "Here's a diet for both of you."

Actually, if the truth be told, a stop sign should have been posted on the refrigerator in January, after Christmas cookie season. It might have been easier to go cold turkey after Christmas turkey than now — the season of ice cream cones and lovely summer pies, and picnics at the beach.

Once I decide to do something, such as quit smoking or lose weight, I can be tough and regimented. The hard part is always getting started.

"No problem," I told MML. "I lost 35 pounds a few years back. This will be a breeze with two of us doing it together. We'll add more exercise, do lots of biking and dog walking and in a week you can call the doctor back and tell him we are ready for Phase II, maintenance, which at least includes frozen yogurt."

I should learn not to brag.

Perhaps middle-age settling is going to take a crane and jack posts to correct. I am not consoled by talk from experts that exercise creates muscle which weighs more than fat. So the fact that I am gaining weight on the austerity diet should not be of concern.

I want results on the scale.

MML, as an incentive, made a graph chart posting our daily results.

His graph looks like a population decline in Southwest Florida in summer as winter visitors dash back North in caravans.

31

Mine resembles the topography of Oklahoma. A minor decline at the start, then flat.

"Men lose weight faster than women," say my friends in their consolations.

That is no cause of solace. MML will be back to Dove Bars by Saturday while I'll still be eating celery during the Christmas holidays.

Perhaps it is my scales. Maybe they are not calibrated with his. I know those at the doctor's office are always set higher than home scales. And because I am also wearing clothing at the medical weigh-in, the picture is even more bleak on my permanent medical record.

I have hung black cloth over all my mirrors until I reach my goal. I have posted pictures of pigs on all temptations — from my favorite stash of peanut butter to the dog's biscuits.

And I try to think "up." I attempt to think positively about what good this is doing me: the extra years I will add to my life; the fact that my relatively new clothes (since the Big Diet of 1982) will fit again.

I comfort myself with the thought that muscle is healthier than fat even if I weigh more now that I am thinner.

I remind myself that having supper constantly in my thoughts during the day is better than worrying about paying bills or whether or not it will ever cool off again.

I tell myself that in our daily new exercise program we are seeing parts of our community we didn't know existed.

We are also learning about new products, such as frozen juice bars with 14 calories.

Our old dogs are getting the exercise of their lives as they try to keep pace with us.

But I can talk myself out of how great this is just as quickly when I remember potato chips, bagels and Betty's Fresh Peach Pie with Raspberry Topping.

Maybe I should consider dessert tonight and a new larger-size wardrobe as an alternative plan.

No, I can be firm in my resolve. Pass the phone cord, please, and hold the mayo.

Dog Guilt

I knew the vacuum cleaner wasn't in the refrigerator. I knew it as soon as I opened the door. And I knew there was no caffeinated brew in the copy machine at work — as soon as I took my mug for a refill.

Lately my mind has been distracted by some major problems in life which tend to keep me from concentrating on all the little things. I have new worries, such as dealing with "blended pet families" and how to keep everyone happy — everyone being two old dogs, each of which is accustomed to being an only child. It is essential to my new romance that our dogs make some sort of adjustment. It keeps one or both of us from suffering from *dog guilt*.

Dog guilt is a feeling of nagging uneasiness brought on by leaving one or the other canine companion alone for lengths of time during which both Mature Adults socialize. Formerly much of that time was spent exclusively in the company of The Dog.

I have had long and futile talks with My Dog. I explain that if he would only stop growling, we could all go for rides together in the car. The four of us. Maybe even for ice cream. My Dog readily promises to behave, but, unfortunately, has almost immediate lapses of memory when he sees Other Dog.

Our problems are compounded by the fact that Other Dog is deaf. Stone deaf. My Dog's throaty growls are a wasted effort. Other Dog, a black cocker spaniel, consistently greets My Dog with great enthusiasm. He is always glad to see his new best friend. That is because he can't hear what My Dog is saying to him (it isn't very nice).

We remove all tennis balls, rawhide chews and bones of contention from their mutual floor space only to find that My Dog has become suddenly possessive of the black, wooden rocking chair and Fluffy the Cat. Other Dog thinks it is a new game and wants to play.

My Dog guards the piano, garbage, vacuum and Christmas presents. He showed his pettiness by opening presents (mine, not his) when I was out of the house. He continues to tear up my mail and raid my laundry. Other Dog isn't even around to wag in appreciation at such a rampage.

Once, on a walk, I thought they were getting along. Then Other Dog lost his head in a moment of friendliness, a gesture instantly misinterpreted. My Dog growled back and I reminded him of his vow to be more cordial. He said he meant to, but forgot, so how about ice cream anyway?

I have moments of forgetfulness too, so I know I must be tolerant of his. I'm still not sure why I thought the vacuum had been stored among the carrots and eggs.

Part of my problem is the distraction of dog relations. My other excuse is that since the children moved Up North, during the last couple years I have had the entire house to myself, except for those territories claimed by my wiry four-legged companion.

There is too much undesignated space. After all these years of vying with children for every inch of floor or cupboard, I technically am sole proprietor of three closets, a pantry, broom closet, stove top and counter tops and table tops, and I tend to use them all.

As a result, there is more than one place something might be, and the challenge of finding it provides occasional exercise.

Maybe the dog is suffering from the same territorial spread. I caught him looking for the squeeze toy in the clean laundry. Perhaps if we re-designated space he'd let me guard the rocker for a while when company visits again.

Sourdough for Starters

There are some gifts, as they say, that just keep on giving.

Man in My Life, who has a fine reputation as a cook, received just such a present from a thoughtful friend during the holidays.

It now requires as much responsibility as remembering to take pills, feed canaries or water plants. Or raise children.

I'm glad it was a gift to him and not me, although I had my chance years ago to try to maintain a similar gift of sourdough starter.

The idea behind the starter is this. Someone who is tired of the rigid schedule of stirring and adding things to it gives it to someone else, along with a tasty loaf of homemade bread and detailed instructions.

"Boy, this would be good to make, and so handy, too," say the starter recipients, sampling the finished product. They feel honored that they have been entrusted with starter of their own.

Of course, they don't know what they are getting themselves into, any more than an unsuspecting person who receives a chain letter. These recipients have no idea how much work is involved to be eligible for a million dollars or postcards or recipes from every country in the world within a month if they merely send off 30 copies to the top names on the list within two days. If the chain is broken, bad luck and misfortune are sure to follow.

Sourdough starter is the chain letter of the food world.

Upon receiving this gift, Man in My Life read the directions carefully and got up extra early on day three and five to stir his starter.

On the 10th day he dutifully added flour and baked two loaves of bread as directed, and tried to share the starter with those to whom he gave the bread.

"We don't have time for sourdough," said one working couple. "We received a yogurt-maker for Christmas and our kitchen is filled with culture."

"I'm a single mother," said another friend. "I can't take any more responsibility."

We were stuck with the starter and had a terrible fear of not keeping it alive.

I remembered what had happened to mine when I moved to Florida.

Friends in Central New York presented me with a loaf of their delicious bread and a small plastic container.

They said, as I packed children and pets in the car, that the starter would be a reminder of them as I settled into my new home.

I misplaced the directions and failed to carry a spoon with me in the car. By the time we arrived at our new abode, the starter had as much life to it as clay, and an odor that rivaled northern New Jersey on a humid day.

I buried it among the palmettos.

But I may have been fortunate that my starter died without a fight. In our efforts to share, others have told us tales of horror about uncontrolled starter dough, rising from its container and spreading like lava.

A gourmet cook from Toronto said that, not understanding the potential hazards of her starter, she left it in the trunk of her car one warm summer day — actually for several days. She forgot about the container and its contents. When she opened the trunk, she discovered it was coated with white frothy dough.

She was among those who have turned us down for some of our new-found yeast treasure.

Despite his attention to it, MML has his problems with the starter.

He forgot to stir one day and found it creeping out over his kitchen counter.

And at times the dough seems sickly and he must resort to emergency measures to resuscitate it.

I am wondering just how to thank the donor of this special gift. Obviously, we can not give her some back. She either has her hands full with her own supply or has cleverly disposed of all of it during the holiday season.

And besides, does culinary etiquette allow for returning starter if one can not care for it properly?

And what if it dies, despite our best efforts? Do we owe the donor an explanation? How can we give her a good excuse, without sounding like we are asking for more from the mother lode?

And what arrangements must we make when we go on vacation? It is hard enough finding places for our pets to stay.

And if we decide to do the unthinkable, to heartlessly rid ourselves of this responsibility, are there environmental rules about not dumping starter dough in the landfill or in a septic system?

Maybe we should leave it in a basket on a church doorstep.

Oh, to turn back the clock to those carefree, guilt-free days before the bread kit arrived. . . .

Three Flush Frogs

Tourists in southwest Florida have been greeted by more than a cold spell. The director of the county office of emergency management has issued heavy frog warnings and forecasts of the Lizard of '89.

It is not welcome news for visitors from New Jersey who had their first frog encounter 30 minutes after unpacking their boots and mittens in the South.

They escaped the big freeze Up North to find themselves in the big freeze, Florida style. The frog did not help matters.

It was, in fact, a three-flush frog. My friend from New Jersey did not believe it was a real frog in the guest room toilet. She thought she was a victim of a practical joke at the hands of her adult cousin. He has a family history of instigating memorable events.

So when she saw the large, whitish frog in the bowl, she assumed the best. She figured it was a plastic, dime store model. She would teach her host a lesson. She would say nothing.

The frog bobbed in the bowl through three flushes before it stretched its long, rubbery legs and began climbing to safety.

The New Jersey visitor hopped backwards into the living room, babbling words known only to people who live within 50 miles of New York City.

The Floridians crossed their fingers and assured her that frogs were a rarity at this time of year, and that perhaps this one was a stowaway in her luggage.

We didn't tell her that nearly everyone who has spent more

than 24 hours in this state has a frog story to tell, and that it is unlikely that it is about the same frog.

Others find lizards in odd places. Odd places are defined as those where lizards do not belong, such as in a house, in a drawer or on top of a lamp or Christmas tree.

The cold weather and/or rain only occurs when we are having company or when we were company.

My winter visits to Florida prior to moving here years ago caused the skies to cloud over immediately and the temperature to drop 40 degrees.

As sleet was forecast along the canals, I huddled in my bathing suit near a smudge pot. My winter coat and gloves were a frosty breath away. I was determined to go home with "color." It was February or March and I was on vacation in Florida, a treat for someone from Central New York.

I chopped ice from my parents' pool to have my picture taken in the water.

I went to the store in shorts and sandals, noticing that only people with Northern plates on their cars were similarly dressed.

I was a good sport. And now, so was the company from New Jersey, once they recovered from the frog shock.

"Where did it come from?" New Jersey asked.

There was no point in telling her that Florida frogs are made of a rubbery substance which enables them to slide under any door or go through tiny holes in screens, then reshape themselves once in the house.

And there was no need to give her the idea that green frogs climb walls and windows, get dizzy at heights of more than six feet and fall accidentally on a person sleeping below.

Why worry her with the idea that once inside a car, a frog has no sense of direction when it hops? Its erratic behavior is not intentional. It does not mean to land on a driver's head.

It was just as well that the temperature plummeted to freezing during the visit. The foreign weather became a distraction from the wildlife seeking refuge indoors.

I, however, did not mind the cold. It was a mini-change of seasons for those of us who still remember the names of three others besides "summer."

I wore my sweaters. All of them at once. It gave me a chance to see if my heating system worked and to let the ceiling fans rest. They have been going for nearly a year without stopping.

The cold spell also provided a new topic of casual conversation around town.

"Sure is cold," replaced, "Nice day, again, huh?"

And the frog alert went out to all households expecting company.

The winter frog crop has arrived. But from what I gather, there isn't much of a market for them in New Jersey. My friends declined to take home any of our live, green souvenirs.

A Dental Appointment
Loses Its Bite

A long-held theory of mine is that if you leave your teeth alone, cavities will heal themselves.

Unfortunately, the American Dental Association has yet to endorse it, along with my suggestions for alternate practical uses for floss. I'll admit my theory is one of my many excuses for not going to the dentist on an even semi-regular basis.

Let me say at the outset, that my aversion to all things dental is nothing personal. My dentist, a wonderful man, with a wonderful staff, would like to see me twice a year in his office.

However, I figure every two years is a close enough compromise. Twice a decade would be more to my liking.

I used to see my name on the missing person list at the post office, as a reminder that it was time to go back in to have my teeth cleaned — something I hate as much as the drill. I see no difference in the experience, except perhaps the bill. For years the dental office called and begged, and I dodged and evaded. It was quite a sport.

But when I hadn't had my usual reminder, I became worried that they had given up the chase. How could I periodically write about my trip to the dentist if my files were marked "closed — married, changed her name and moved"?

"Hmm," said the receptionist, "I can see that you were due back to have a filling fixed two years ago. . ."

"Give them time and they repair themselves," I said.

"People are too quick to rush in for the extra silver in their mouths these days," I added, hoping for a good pre-examination discussion. There was none. They had obviously had a staff meeting about patients such as me and decided to play it real cool, not rising to our bait. No fun at all.

The fact that I had booked the appointment myself without a subpoena from the surgeon general should have caught my dentist by surprise. Always before, his staff had to think of creative ruses to lure me in.

"Are you here because you are having a problem?" the dentist asked as he held my X-rays to the light.

"Nope. The reason I am here is simple: I don't want to puff up and die," I said.

"I am your dentist, not a balloonist," said he.

So I told him what I had heard at breakfast after church the other morning. Some friends told me that a cousin had puffed up and died because she didn't get her teeth cleaned. I had the impression it was generally puffing — whole body puffing — not localized to her face.

I am having enough trouble with my diet. No need to puff up more for lack of dental work.

Since it had been two years since my last appointment, I figured there was a message in there somewhere.

To top it off, old Fluffy's face puffed up like a beach ball. I thought she had been in a cat fight. A trip to the vet last week proved otherwise. Her face was swollen like a prize fighter because of abscessed teeth. It could be fatal. My second warning.

"So, that's why I'm here today," I said, "because I don't want to look like Fluffy, spend the night at the vet and eat chopped tuna."

"I see," he said. "Open wider."

Fluffy isn't the only member of the family who has had her teeth worked on lately.

We seem to be having a stream of bad dental luck. Both dogs had their teeth cleaned. Dog biscuits are no longer sufficient to purge their choppers.

They were lucky enough to get a total anesthetic. My dentist doesn't believe in that.

Man in My Life wanted to make sure that if his dog had gleaming teeth, his breath would be sweet for at least a week and that the old fellow would live long enough for us to pay off the loan needed to pay the canine dental bill. However, the shine did not come with a guarantee of any sort.

"Everything looks just fine," said my dentist. He didn't ask if I flossed. He didn't remind me to brush. In fact, he didn't mention the cavity that needed filling two years ago. How could I bolt from the room, saying, "Catch me if you can," before they tried to schedule my follow-up appointment?

His lack of interest was making me nervous.

"But what about my cavity? What about it? You said it had to be filled? And what about my wisdom teeth that you said had to come out three years ago? I still haven't flossed. Don't you care?"

"Oh yes, the cavity. I suppose I might find the time to take care of it if you really want it done. Just beg me for an appointment on the way out," said my dentist.

"How soon can you take me?" I asked the receptionist. "This tooth might start hurting. It needed attention two years ago. . . . I should have taken care of it long ago."

"Let me see. I have nothing for a month," she said.

"I'll take it. Just don't ignore me. I can't stand it. I want to be a Mature Adult."

My appointment card is carefully taped on the wall by my desk.

As I contemplate it, I wonder, with the dentist's staff changing their tactics, who won. In the new game, the victory is theirs. I don't like being a Mature Adult.

A Crash Course in Kittens

My mother always said that kittens grow up to be cats. I can't wait.

She used that as an excuse for not having kittens in our home. She claimed to find them appealing but just didn't like the adult version.

I never thought I would say this: I'm looking forward to the day when our twin adolescent felines grow up, become fat and lazy, and just lie around doing nothing. It is the *doing-nothing* part that I am especially waiting for.

Our "girls" are three months old. In cat years, that is age 15 — the heart of teen-age trouble.

They leave the room, but don't say where they are going. They constantly try to go into parts of the house where they don't belong.

They know right from wrong, but do what they please with sweet, blank expressions. They climb screens, shred potted plants (both live and artificial), tread where cats are not supposed to tread, and use the pool without permission.

Why can't cats be more like dogs? Dogs don't climb drapes.

We have tried to keep The Kittens out of the living room so they won't be tempted to scale the curtains. Of course that is the first place they want to visit each time we come home and let them out of the laundry room.

As I was reading last night, I thought I saw them sneak past me.

"Where are The Kittens going?" asked the Man in My Life.

"Now that you mention it, I think they went through the door to the living room."

We dashed in after them to rescue the curtains and figurines.

No kittens in view. I looked under the couch and behind the chairs.

Invisible kittens. I called them in my nicest kitten voice. We searched and called, but no kittens anywhere.

Suddenly, there was the giveaway sneeze.

A dusty kitten face emerged from under a cupboard. No contrition. And no cooperation. When I try to pick up a kitten who does not want to go with me, she becomes limp and heavy. I need

44

a spatula.

Why can't kittens be more like canaries and stay in one place?

During this time of maturation, their hunting skills are reaching perfection. They stalk ants and study squadrons of dragonflies, while planning an attack.

They have fallen into the pool. Man in My Life claims he did not push one in when he came up behind it. He says he was going to pick it up but she fell in the deep end. Before we could say "Ding dong dell, pussy's in the well," the young cat shot out of the pool like a missile, landing back on the deck. Her water maneuver occurred so quickly that MML called me over to touch her. It was astounding. Her tabby coat was not even wet.

Why can't kittens be more like hamsters?

Their curiosity is not doing them as much harm as it is the rest of us. I have risked several of my nine lives to see what has caused various crashes in the house.

A particularly loud, metallic *thwunk!* came from the family room, near MML's favorite chair.

One young cat had miscalculated a leap from the chair to an end table, catching a decorative tabletop pad in her frantic claws. Pad, toothpicks, nail clipper, channel changer, pen, calculator and surprised kitten all landed in a metal wastebasket.

Despite my parental counsel, The Kittens insist on walking on tops of things, spinning our Lazy Susan free of spices and scattering magazines on the floor.

What's a mother to do? The dogs at least show remorse for a few minutes, when caught in the act of bad behavior. Not so the cats.

I'm not saying that all dogs are good and that cats are bad. I'm just less of a judge of cats. And since these are the children of a stray cat who had found our back yard in time for babies, it is hard to evaluate the effects of prenatal influence.

I thought they would be so happy to have a good home and tasty treats that they would be forever grateful and mind their manners. I wasn't prepared for these wild teen times at a time in my life when the last of my teens is in college.

MML is enjoying their antics. He says kittens will be kittens. After that last crash, I want to know when they will be more like cats.

Read My Hips...

Cookies are screaming at me. Corn chips hurl themselves at my feet from convenience store shelves. I have developed an unprecedented craving for ice cream and raspberry pie — all since I decided to be a little more conservative in my eating after the holidays.

I hesitate to call my regimen a formal diet. That would lock me into something which requires special recipes and calorie counting. However, it will end up that way if my less formal effort at mere common sense and sheer willpower is not successful immediately.

It is not the first time I have tried to hold the line on what I shall euphemistically call flab. I gained a significant amount of weight when I quit smoking about 15 years ago. I gained 30 pounds sucking three leaves of crisp, green iceberg lettuce. The sirens' song of peanut butter cookies is compelling right now. I hear my name every time I pass them.

So this year's holiday overindulgence caused me to do two things: throw out my scales (too depressing to use) and resolve to be more careful before February candy arrives.

But it didn't help. I must buy a new wardrobe or hire a full-time seamstress for alterations. I maintained the same nice weight for so many years since my last very strict diet that I had lulled myself into complacency. I believed I was invincible to the detrimental effects of six stuffed pastry puffs, along with other *hors d'oeuvres.* I believed I was pudge-proof.

This year was my downfall. There wasn't a night between Thanksgiving and New Year's that some treat or feast didn't tempt me. I tried to rationalize my behavior at the buffet tables by thinking that my gain might be someone else's loss. But the proof was in the pudding, plum or otherwise.

Even though I am going at this effort in what I consider a common sense approach — eliminating all the things I like from meals and eating moderately, only three times a day, and skipping the fun stuff altogether — what I am "missing" preoccupies my waking thoughts.

As I drive around the county, I realize how many restaurants there are and where all the opportunities for ice cream, frozen yogurt and bagels exist.

I crave every candy in the dish on the counter of the quick-print shop, even if I don't like the flavor.

I find myself staring at other people's food and making many much-too-casual inquiries about how people enjoyed their lunch and what they had and asking if there were leftovers.

I am consumed with the desire to read food sections of newspapers and wonder if it really takes a three-hour brisk walk to work off one doughnut (or is that a Jane Fonda scare tactic?).

I try to convince myself that fruit is better for me than wonderful Christmas cookies. And one of these days, when I lose five pounds, I may believe it if I say it often enough.

Fruit is better than sugar cookies. Fruit is better than sugar cookies hot from the oven. Fruit is better than a dozen sugar cookies hot from the oven and decorated with little green and red crystals. Fruit is . . .

Nothing Worse Than Fruitcake

I'm in fruitcake shock. Two friends said they actually like it. I'm afraid to stand under the mistletoe with them.

A third likes it conditionally. The condition is that she can pick out the stuff she doesn't like. By the time she finished describing what needed to be excavated from the cake, all that was left is the rum.

Fruitcake is a much-discussed Christmas present. In a national survey of worst gifts, it even placed behind receiving "nothing at all."

The pollsters didn't ask me, but apparently my opinion, for once, is in the mainstream.

Fruitcake lovers I located assume my dislike of this unpleasant holiday confection stems from an unfortunate experience as a child, or even as a middle-aged adult. They think that my diatribe against fruitcake must be based on a bad sample I once ingested.

Perhaps I have blocked out such an encounter. But, in reality, I don't think I ever tasted a fruitcake at all. And I am not about to try. On my list of worst possible experiences, along with plumbing backing up before the arrival of a large crowd of weekend guests from Buffalo, is unwanted fruitcake surprise.

That refers to my anxiety, my fear of being in a smoke-filled room, unable to see what is on the snack plate at a large public gathering, and having my hand slip from its target of crisp carrot sticks and accidentally grasp a piece of the dreaded cake.

Then, just as I am to be introduced to the President of the United States, the first unexpected bite would numb my lips and my tongue would recoil at the nuggets of citron — clear bullets of bitter flavor — a veritable mine field for unwary taste buds.

Would I be able to conduct an intelligent conversation about federal flood insurance for the barrier islands or interstate highway systems?

I'm afraid not. The nation's leader would pass me by to converse with someone spreading American-made cheese balls on "safe" crackers. Then I would probably be pressed by the hostess to have a second piece of fruitcake, or be forced to take the rest home as a Christmas treat.

Someone who loves fruitcake — even one bite, once a year — has no idea of the trauma involved for those of us who are not blessed by visions of fruitcake dancing in our heads.

A fruitcake to them is little different than a chocolate cake or a piece of fudge, or a lovely apple pie from New England.

My theory is that as children they suffered irreversible damage by holding their breath and turning blue when they were denied a pony. As a result, they lost their ability to sort out flavors — good ones from bad.

They like other things, like squid and brussels sprouts.

And if they had the option, they would make a cake of squid and brussels sprouts and hand it out at Christmas and expect to see smiles of thanks.

As much as I have tried to consider the merits of fruitcake, I have come up with none. There is more to be said in favor of brussels sprouts, but you don't see them gift wrapped for Christmas. Maybe the purpose of fruitcake is to make everything else look good. It works.

Does It Take Two to Mango?

On June 17 at 7:30 a.m., I sampled a mango. I not only tasted a mango, I tried to like it.

After 11 years of living in Florida, it seemed appropriate to my on-going adjustment. Besides, I was out of grapefruit for breakfast.

My bold, if you will, moment with the fruit originated more from guilt than a spirit of culinary adventure.

I have two large mango trees in my side yard. Outer Mangolia resembles a battlefield with undetonated orange bombs.

For lack of rain, local talk concerns the unusually abundant crop this year. A few heavy rainstorms should turn conversational pleasantries to mosquitoes and overflowing swales.

My trees have had little fruit until now — so little they might be mistaken for some other variety of native vegetation such as hibiscus.

But suddenly the mangoes arrived in a veritable "blizzard." There was no time to signal the start of its season. They wake the dog as they crash over the kitchen roof and land in the cat's bowl.

"Waste not, want not," was something I was taught. It should *not* be applied to mangoes.

I can't see what the appeal is. Had my trees borne one fruit, that would have been more than enough.

Surprisingly, people are actually asking me for them.

In fact, one native says he loves the pithy turpentine variety I own. He noticed our bountiful crop and called for his share.

"Take as many as you want," I urged. "They are all over the place and are getting black spots."

"That's when they are the best," he said. "They are ripe."

Each to his own. I don't even like bananas with black spots.

Why couldn't mangoes be grapefruit? Now there is something every yard should have — as many grapefruit this time of year as I have in unwanted tropical fruit. I am a Northerner with northern taste buds. The things I like to eat, such as tomatoes and citrus, never make it to harvest in my garden.

Back North, we had four old fruit trees in our city yard. We had two green apple trees, suitable only for climbing. Their unedible produce was handy weaponry in the hands of my son when he was five.

And we had pear and plum. Every other year there was enough to harvest for jams or canning from those two ancient trees.

I had my heart set on plum jelly one year; bought my pectin, sugar and jelly jars and watched the tree each day for the perfect morning to harvest the crop.

The day before the perfect morning, I was all ready to go, and made my plans to begin plum picking and jelly making by dawn's early light.

Bushel basket in hand, I stood under the tree. There was not a plum left. Not one. My immediate suspicions turned to neighborhood children who must have climbed the fence and made off with my harvest by the light of the moon.

Then I discovered another clue. Hundreds of pits on the ground. The children had a feast, I figured.

But the culprits were soon discovered: a pair of very adolescent raccoons, probably with quite a bellyache for their gluttonous thievery.

Where are the raccoon twins now when I need them? Even the squirrels have not consumed their share of mangoes.

I have enough mangoes to feed the third world tons of fruit salad.

The Mature Adult response to such a bumper crop should be to learn to fix and eat mangoes, rather than let them rot.

So, as a sign of maturity, I selected one with appropriate black spots for breakfast.

Unsure of the next step, we peeled it and made an effort to slice the next layer which looks like wet, orange macramé.

We put the mushy "slices" on a small plate between the cereal bowls.

"Who's going to try it first?" I asked cheerfully.

Failing to convince anyone else, I sampled one bite. It was not what I expected. Or maybe it was. One bite was enough. And no one else joined me.

Maybe it takes more than one to appreciate its flavor. Perhaps it takes two to mango.

Forever Bad

"You will forever be my bad dog!" said the man from Brooklyn.

This horrendous pronouncement was made in front of witnesses at the veterinarian's office. My dog and I both heard it. So did another family with a brown dog.

It was the stuff that finds its way into fairy tales. The brothers Grimm couldn't have said it better.

A white dog wearing a sock over his bandaged foot had disgraced his owner behind his back while the man was paying the receptionist.

As we could readily see, more than a mop was needed. The curse was dramatically repeated: "Forever my bad dog!"

Before our eyes, it began to take effect. The little pooch, instead of being convinced to mend his ways, was damned without hope of redemption. The dog immediately became forever bad. He promptly lifted his leg on the counter when his master again turned to settle the account.

"Forever my bad dog! Why can't you be like all these other good doggies?" asked the owner as he dragged the doomed and unchastened pooch from the waiting room to the car.

And we were there to see it, right there at the animal clinic — a modern "forever" curse working its worst.

One could only imagine how the pair would spend the rest of their lives. What had been a friendly, pedigreed dog willing to wear just one sock, would probably appear in his master's suits and ties, after he had eaten all the shoelaces off his shoes and dug a hole in the couch. He would no doubt stop gamboling and start gambling and smoking. He might become an international terrierist. Forever.

It is odd how these things work. I still can't step on a crack without wondering if it might break my mother's back, and I avoid the under-the-ladder path. It is just too risky. Now I realize that those are more in the category of superstition than curse, but they have the same origin as curses and spells as I remember them from my childhood.

I just emerged from the effects of a spell, so I can talk with some measure of authority.

Here is how it came about. When my mother moved to Florida in 1974 from Long Island, she looked about at all the opportunities for new flora and decided to plant wonderful Southern plants instead of trying to bring the Northern variety with her.

She had gerbera daisies, lychee, avocado, orchids, bird of paradise, hibiscus of many sizes and colors. Her beautiful garden was nouveau Florida.

I said it looked nice, but I personally missed roses and lilacs.

"Roses don't grow in Florida," said my mother, a woman no one argued with (at least not successfully).

I thought I saw roses growing in the next yard. Lots of them. I made the mistake of mentioning them.

"Roses don't grow here at all," said my mother, dispelling the thought.

Occasionally her neighbor, Emily, brought her a rose. Mother put it in a bud vase on the lanai table.

We didn't notice it, nor comment on its fragrance.

I was as convinced as any that all of Florida was roseless, maybe even forever.

The fact that rose bushes were sold at nurseries and at the supermarket checkout did not break the enchantment.

However, as near as I can tell, my mother's spell was of the variety which sunsets after 15 years.

So one day recently I woke up and smelled the roses. All our neighbors have them. Rose bushes across the street. Buds next door. Blooms everywhere. Floribunda. Pink ones, rose red and rose white.

I immediately bought three bushes for my own.

"Look," I said to the Man in My Life, "roses do grow in Florida after all. I wonder if it is something new. . . . . I wish Mother were alive so I could show her."

MML knows when to say nothing, in the face of such powerful magic.

He simply asked where I wanted to plant them.

The white dog has been on my mind. I'm hoping his owner gets some newt's tongues and eyes of potatoes and stir-fries gently while reciting "knick knack paddywhack, give the dog a bone." I've heard it works in other cases.

Forever bad is such a long, long time.

Things That Go Bong in the Night

It's hot. Summer heat has come earlier this year.

It's 1 a.m. and hot. I am awakened by the Dog Boys. They are not barking or defending us. They are snoring. Man in My Life says this chorus goes on every night. He says he feels as if he is sleeping in a dormitory.

The old pets moan in their sleep and sometimes pace from room to room. They shake their jowls. There is no point in banishing them. They will scratch and thump at the bedroom door to be let back in. We've tried it.

It's 2 a.m. The clocks are bonging. All four of them, but not at the same moment. They tick and they bong, and tick and bong some more.

I remember that when we had a puppy, someone once said you should let it sleep with an alarm clock wrapped in a blanket to simulate a mother's heartbeat. I am thinking about wrapping the clocks in blankets. The ticking is not particularly comforting when I want to sleep. At least I will know when it is 3 a.m. I will know it four times. Four times three is 12. Maybe if I practice my times tables it will be like counting sheep. I will bore myself to sleep.

I am staring at the fan circling overhead and thinking that I haven't multiplied anything but clutter and pets in 20 years since I bought my first calculator. I don't remember my times tables.

My calculator is on my desk next to the bills. Specifically, it is next to the phone bill which for some reason is astronomically high this month.

I don't want to think about bills. I'll never get to sleep.

3:30 a.m. and humid. One bong from three clocks. I've been dozing and dreaming that a friend has just gotten word that he is covered with killer head lice. He is supposed to let everybody he has been in contact with know by letter but doesn't have anyone proofread his spelling. The letter is a mess.

The dream reminds me of something else I don't want to remember — the TV movie MML and I were watching earlier in the evening, *Killer Slugs*.

53

In the film, slugs were detected in a Central New York community, not far from where I actually lived years ago. It was just as I expected. Awful mutant slugs in the cellar had the potential to getcha if you didn't watch out. MML said slugs don't really attack and kill and don't grow as big as the movie showed them to be, but what does he (a former science teacher) know? Had he ever seen my cellar?

I don't want to count slugs, either. But it is 4 a.m. and I am desperate enough to consider anything, including trying to think of all the words I can that rhyme with them.

Hugs. I think of my children and how they used to come in and wake me up when they had bad dreams.

Oldest Child was convinced during one such somnambulance that there was an alligator in his bathtub. He insisted that I come check it out. He was so terrified I preferred not to look myself.

In the middle of the night, even in Central New York, all things could be possible, even alligators.

"How about sleeping on the couch in the living room?" I asked as an alternate solution.

"The alligator has fangs and glowing eyes," he cried.

"I think you must just be having a bad dream," I said.

"Then come and prove it," howled the tyke.

"I've got a better idea," I said. "You go back to bed, and we'll both check it out in the morning," I said.

It didn't work. We both slept in the living room. Just as I hoped, by morning the mutant gator was gone.

In retrospect, I'm glad I didn't send him back to his room. That's what people did in the slug movie. They said, "Don't worry dear, just go ahead and fix dinner while I go back to work," and their loved ones were never seen again.

5 a.m. and 20 bongs. The dogs are stirring. They are getting ready to bark at the mutant garbage truck which starts its day on our street.

I am exhausted from trying to remember my times six tables, and marvel that I ever took trigonometry and try to remember what it was about. Perhaps it did prepare me for life, as my math teacher insisted it would. If giant calculator-eating slugs ever took over the world, I'd be in plenty of trouble trying to balance my checkbook if I hadn't taken all that math in high school.

It's still hot. The Dog Boys snore through the garbage truck at 5:30 a.m. I don't.

Nor can I block out the chorus of frogs, which has swelled.
6 a.m. The alarm. I don't hear it. MML wakes me.
"How'd ya sleep, sweetheart?"
"I kept hearing the slugs go tick and bong."
"Never mind, I'll get the coffee . . . It's hot."

Worries Grow on a Gardener

My tomatoes are the envy of the neighborhood, through no fault of mine.

A surrogate gardener has taken over this year's effort. He pitied me as I told my annual tale of woe. Next thing I knew, two healthy potted tomatoes appeared by my front step. And within minutes, he returned with skyscraper-like wire cages to encircle them.

I was impressed and curious.

"What are the cages for?" I asked, wondering if these were some special wandering variety of garden vegetable that needed restraint.

"To keep the bunnies out," said my friend.

Bunnies? In town? Given the height of the wire, I felt reason to be alarmed. I had not seen 6-foot rabbits in my yard, but maybe The Dog had after dark. Maybe they were what he was barking at, not the Possum Express that we thought came through like clockwork at 11 p.m. for a rest stop at the cat's dish.

My friend hid the fertilizer in the bushes. Gallons of it. In all my years of gardening, it had not occurred to me to supplement nature with secret blue tonic.

I believe in survival of the fittest, which usually includes my tomatoes.

"If you leave the plants by the front door, I will water them," said my friend.

55

Water them? A novel idea. Food and water in case Mother Nature's cupboard was bare.

The plants were eight inches tall when they settled into their new life, watching traffic pass on my street.

Within a week, they doubled in height and sprouted yellow flowers, which I resisted the urge to pick for dinner table decorations.

Two weeks later I sent their framed picture to the Grange and asked when the state fair was coming.

And now, all of a sudden, hard little green tomatoes are everywhere. I have rushed to the store to buy canning jars and spaghetti noodles. I am wondering if I should hire someone to do my ironing so my laundry basket can be emptied in time to hold the harvest.

I'm also worried that there is no end to my tomatoes' growth. One is nearly at the top of its pen, in easy reach of the giant rabbits (which may be swigging the tonic when no one is home). The other had a bit of a mishap with some tree limbs. Having lost some of its height, it is developing horizontally at a vigorous pace.

What if the bunnies can't wait for their share to fall over the top, and drive a pick-up truck to my portable garden and take it back to their burrows where they can marvel among themselves at the wondrous properties of the blue tonic?

I had no idea that my garden, even in the hands of someone so competent and experienced, could be such a source of worry.

I wonder if there is time to grow potted carrots as a distraction for the wildlife. They'd do well if the oversized bunnies haven't finished off the tonic. I'll consult the gardener.

Old Dogs and Swimming Pools

The Dog is too embarrassed to talk about this, but he fell in a swimming pool twice Sunday. And given his increasingly portly physique, he needed help getting out.

The first time he miscalculated a few backward steps. The second time he was sleeping on the deck and rolled over. He was not on a water bed, but he found himself in one.

Some of his problems stem from his advancing years. He is a bit forgetful, as are we all. And he is not accustomed to having a pool just a paw-slip away. The pool is at Other Dog's house, where The Dog and I frequently visit.

In all honesty, my dog has had a history of falling adventures since his puppyhood, only they were not always as comfortable an experience as landing in a warm swimming pool with somewhat sympathetic rescuers at hand.

When I was first on my own as a single parent, the children were young and so was The Dog. We decided to take a nice walk in the woods of Skaneateles, New York. The woods were lovely, dark and very deep with ravines and waterfalls and fern-covered cliffs made of little pieces of slippery layered shale.

I was masking my nervousness about taking everyone on this outing as the only responsible adult. I tried to remember what I had learned in summer camp about carrying injured people out of the mountains on litters, Indian style.

If one of the children were treed by a bear, could I rise to the occasion as a good mother, kill the bear, chop the tree down, build a fire and cook marshmallows? It was a lot to be concerned with.

We were hiking down the dry creek bed with The Dog running along the cliff some 30 feet above when a black object fell from the sky at our feet with an ominous thud.

It was The Dog. Flattened. Dead.

Thinking quickly, I knew we would need our belts and jackets and long sticks to make the litter, and become pall bearers.

How awful. I didn't want to be the responsible adult and tell the children the obvious. Their new dog, that they didn't much like because he had weird bloodshot eyes and a wiry coat, was dead on our first field trip together. They would want to go live with their father. He would probably buy them a soft poodle which could walk a tightrope across gorges.

My son, tears trickling down his face, sat next to the lifeless form, petting the bristly head, calling The Dog's name.

"We'll carry him out, and bury him properly," I said, trying to figure out how Indians kept a jacket tied to two sticks with a child's pink plastic belt.

The Dog's tail thumped and he opened one weird eye.

"Don't get your hopes up, son," I said. "He's really a goner. He fell from 30 feet."

More patting and talking.

The Dog staggered to his feet.

"Don't get your hopes up. He's really quite dead. Internal injuries, son. Trust me. A mother knows these things."

The Dog licked my son's hands and shook himself.

"Help me lift him onto this jacket. We'll drag him back up the cliff to the car."

The Dog trotted down the creek bed, sniffing the rocks.

"It's hopeless. We'll get a soft poodle that can walk tight ropes," I said.

The Dog ran up a path and bolted into the woods after a deer.

"We'll find his body any minute. Prepare yourselves. Poodles are quite nice."

We found The Dog, dirty and wagging next to the car. Just as I had thought.

Two years ago, while on an unauthorized lizard-chasing expedition he fell into a canal. He growled at would be rescuers until they gave him a ladder, a meal and a warm bath.

I had reported him missing to the police department, who in turn relayed my name to those who had saved him.

"Black and white, overweight and has weird eyes," I said.

"Not good enough. How many collars did he have on," asked the finders, who wanted a complete description.

Not only was I guilty of not knowing where my dog was that Saturday afternoon, but I failed the big identification test. He had two collars. I forgot about his flea collar. I was lucky to get him back under those conditions.

Maybe he was remembering his moments of glorious adventure — of his earlier nine lives — when he slid into the pool.

I'm glad the kids weren't around to see how foolish he looked

... or to hear me yell "dog overboard, start building a raft." I think that's what I learned about water rescues in summer camp.

Promises to Love, Honor and Keep
Less Clutter

Somewhere among all the boxes left to be unpacked since the move is the mail which was on my kitchen counter in my other house.

Mostly it includes letters that needed to be answered. One, not opened, is from a high school classmate. I have a sneaky suspicion it contains information about our 30th reunion, but since I can't find that pile of highly important documents, I may never know.

Man in My Life, a neat and orderly person, chronically suggests that my kitchen counters are not the appropriate place for mail. He says the space should be used for cooking. Each to his own. I was living between freezer and microwave before he came into my life.

He puts bills and letters and such in pigeon holes in his desk and has important papers systematically filed in well-marked manila folders. As I said, each to his own.

I am a pile, rather than file, person. Mine is a vertical system which has served me well through the years. There is no expenditure at the office supply store for metal cabinets and decorative filing systems. My way is cost-efficient and environmentally sound. An added benefit is that furniture never needs dusting. It has a permanent cover. And because I save so many important papers, I have not exceeded my quota at the landfill.

But in my marriage vows, I promised to love, honor and compromise on clutter.

While my writing room is disarranged with my traditional organizational system, the rest of the house is organized and monitored by MML. In return, he has promised never to say a word, never gasp in dismay, never clutch his throat and choke at what he observes in my own little corner of the world.

He even helped set it all up for me: the tangle of computer wires, the piles of newspapers, the overstuffed bookshelves. And then he tiptoed back into the orderly world beyond, making some untranslatable noises.

What I had not realized was that one member of the animal kingdom who dwells with us likes my new desk arrangement.

Fluffy the Cat took one look at the nest of clutter and decided it was her place to roost. She especially likes the computer printer near the window. I find her curled up on the paper feeder, surveying her new neighborhood.

I didn't know she would also do some typing. Unfortunately, she used the keyboard without telling me.

I thought it was broken. Every time I tried to type my column, I saw a combination of numbers and letters where words should be. It looked like this: 16145k4d th46.

In dismay, I made arrangements for a loaner, and called data processing to let them know my unit was on the way back for a tuneup. I described the problem.

There was a thoughtful silence at the other end of the line.

"Release the 'num' key," said my rescuer.

"Release the what?" I said.

"The number key. When it is pushed in, you get numbers mixed with your letters."

I don't know why they put such things on keyboards, especially where cats can step on them on their way to a nesting spot.

Why would anyone, except spies, want to type in a code which is a combination of letters and numbers?

How was I to know my keyboard wasn't broken? Do I look like someone who is computer-apt?

I tried the computer-whiz's suggestion and mumbled "darn cat" in the phone.

"What?" said Data Processing.

"I was just remembering the days of manual typewriters, when the worst thing a cat could do was step on all the keys and cause an alphabet pile-up on the platen roller."

Actually I had a flashback to high school typing class. The boys in the prior period had discovered that the key caps were removable. So they removed and changed them around on the keyboard.

I, struggling to learn the non-logical location of the alphabet, typed "g" and "f" would appear, and so on. When I tried to explain my predicament to Miss Gibbs, she was silent and gave me a look of disbelief down through her granny glasses.

I guess it was good preparation for life. Somehow I did learn to touch-type that semester. As I reflect philosophically, I now know that writers must learn to cope with the pranks of boys and cats. However, Fluffy is banished from the writing room. She is *catis non gratis* on the computer clutter table.

Teacher Takes a Driving Lesson

Who taught my daughter to drive like a cabbie?

When she took lessons from Mom's School of Defensive Driving, she learned to wait for every other motorist to pass through town before venturing past an intersection. She learned that big trucks always have the right of way.

She learned that just because it is green doesn't mean that you should go. That decision is best made after looking both ways at the guys whose light shows red.

She learned to observe the speed limits, keep her eyes on the road, not to chew gum or eat a hamburger at the wheel. Stuff like that.

Her first few evening lessons were spent in the parking lot of First Baptist Church. We slowly circled the building until the rehearsing choir was dizzy.

Middle Child cried when she heard the news that there was more to driving than an empty church lot.

"Don't be afraid, just look both ways, shift into second, use your blinker and let's ease out onto Gill Street," I said.

"That's good. Just use the clutch not the brake next time. And keep your eyes open."

For a very shy person, driving through a nearby upscale development the first time was scary. Especially if there was another car coming towards us. It might even be her grandmother.

What if she forgot how to stick shift at the stop sign and her grandmother was watching? What if she went through a stop sign and somebody in a blue and white car was watching? What if she just wanted to go home and have milk and cookies and hold Big Baby, her favorite doll?

It took us another month to get up the courage to try parallel parking, and three weeks of practice before she was willing to attempt it between cars.

We practiced on every side street in town, all the back roads out of town, and graduated to U.S. 41 in time to pass the driver's test.

And pass she did. Carefully. Cautiously. The way adults like to see our youth of today drive.

So where did she learn to merge from eight lanes of Boston traffic into a two-lane tunnel at rush hour and force big trucks to wait for her little compact?

Shy daughter at the wheel in city traffic. A case for the next edition of "Ripley's Believe it or Not."

When she offered to drive me from her apartment on the trip to Boston, it had not occurred to me that she knew her way around. I've never lived there. So why should my daughter manage without a map?

She whizzed through expressway traffic like a pro and negotiated exits and interchanges as if she had been born in the Commonwealth itself.

I closed my eyes briefly — not to relax, but because I didn't want to look.

"Tell me when we are in the parking garage," I begged, after taking one look at the looming Tunnel Merge.

That type of traffic situation would have been enough to draw a television station into our little county for the evening news coverage.

"This is how it always is in Boston," said shy child, boldly inching her new car between a laundry truck and a cement mixer as the drivers honked and yelled.

"Don't you care that they won't like you?" I said, smiling and waving back.

"Mommmm . . ."

In my heart, as bad as traffic is in the winter in Florida, I suddenly realized that by comparison we live in bucolic America.

My formerly sheltered child seemed to enjoy the challenge of forcing the trucks to stall as she crept ahead of a limo, two pickups and three foreign cars as well.

"How do you know it is your turn to go?" I asked. "Shouldn't you give someone else a turn and be nice?"

"Where would you like to eat, Mom?" was her response.

"Excuse us, please," I mouthed to an irate taxi driver.

At the point at which a bus moved out of her way, I would have abandoned the car and hitchhiked back to Southwest Florida rather than contend with driving through the tunnel myself. Where did she learn such assertive skills?

Not only does she do tunnel traffic, she can drive in sleet and snow. She can park on a hill and drive to Vermont alone.

Secretly, I am proud. Secretly, I also know that she doesn't need me . . . at least to help her parallel park anymore. She is leading a life of her own. She checks her own oil.

If only the Baptist choir could see her now. They might want to hire her as a bus driver for their next tour north.

Moms in the Shadows

Yes, Virginia, there is night life in our county, which had a false reputation as a place which closes down at 6 p.m., right after the early bird specials at local restaurants. Obviously those who claim there is no activity after dark south of New York have not been to the parking lot of the movie theater on a Friday night.

"You went to the movies on a Friday?" several people (two of them were teen-agers) asked me and my friend incredulously.

"That's when all the junior high kids hang out there," they said.

It was true. From a distance we thought we would have to wait in a long line to see our show. The crowd was thick. We were afraid we had dawdled over dinner too long and would not be able to get in.

But there was no line at all, once we got to the theater, despite the fact there were two new movies advertised on the billboard.

We found a sea of kids, milling and talking and playing radios. A few were buying tickets to roam inside where it was air conditioned. Others were just there.

I think every person in the county between the ages of 11 and 17 had gathered to socialize.

It made me miss Youngest Child, who has not been home for a while. It was her kind of place.

I remembered the time she and I went to the movies there on another Friday night several seasons ago. It was an unusual occurrence for us.

She had been unable to come up with appropriate evening plans with her peers. So there was nothing to do and no one to do nothing with. I offered to take her to a show. Surprisingly, she accepted. We even agreed on the movie.

She was 15. I thought it would be lovely for The Mother and The Youngest Child to spend an evening doing something together. It was the sort of togetherness opportunity that mothers of young teens fantasize about — taking their teen-ager somewhere without the entire eighth grade or sophomore class, and then having a pleasant conversation.

Youngest Child rarely was willing to be seen in public with me — just at a shopping mall when we met at the cashier's station.

So I figured the movies would be lots of fun. We could sit

together and share a tub of popcorn and poke each other during the funny parts. Dr. Spock would want to hear about it for his next book on communicating with teens.

Once inside the theater complex we located our show and sat together with our buttery treat. For five minutes. She spotted some friends in the front row, dashed off to join them and before the title had finished rolling across the screen, the expanding group had left our little corner of cinema world.

By the time I caught up with her in the lobby after the movie, she had seen bits and pieces of six shows, and had exchanged phone numbers with two new friends and made plans to invite 20 people over to the house for a cookout on her next birthday.

They had all accepted, assuming I would be willing to be inconspicuous as a mother figure.

I certainly was out of the way at the movies. No one knew I had come with a teen-ager.

"Let's do this again sometime," said Youngest Child.

Then she added, "I told everyone I would meet them at McDonald's. Can I borrow some money? You can come in, Mom, as long as you don't act like you're my mom."

Fine with me. I didn't mind sitting alone in a fast food place filled with teens at 10 p.m. with an empty popcorn tub over my head. Not at all. That was what family togetherness is all about.

"Hi," said a helpful child who had been at our house frequently. "Jenny's sitting over there, didn't you see her?"

"I'm not supposed to know her," I replied. "And I don't know if I am supposed to know you either, Andrea. You'd better not be seen talking to me. It could be bad for your reputation.

"We're just having a fun night out together, Jen and I," I said. "If you want to be really helpful, slip this note to my kid and tell her to either meet me by the car in five minutes or get a live-in job at the theater."

I looked at the faces of the young teens as we passed them Friday, and wondered where they had hidden their mothers. I figured they were somewhere inside, alone ... with a fresh popcorn tub for two.

The Curse of
the Bathroom Frog

Just as I suspected. Frogs are out to get me. I suppose there are some of you who do not believe that these green creatures have enough gray matter to be considered cunning. Nor do you think they bite. Just let me ask you this. Just how well do you know your frogs?

The most recent episode of insidious frog behavior caused me to be locked out of my house the next night.

"I don't understand the connection," said Man in My Life. It was the first communication crisis in our 17-day-old marriage.

"How can you say the frog we found in *my* house on Wednesday night, caused you to pick up the wrong keys and be locked out of *your* house on Thursday night?" he asked a bit incredulously.

"Does this mean the honeymoon is over?" I said. "You don't believe me?"

"It's not that I don't believe you. I just don't understand the connection."

"I was thinking about the frog instead of my car keys. So I picked up the wrong set — the one with just the car keys on it. As soon as I got outside and closed the door, the frog's grinning face vanished and the image of my real keys, on the dining room table where I left them, appeared."

"I see," said MML, not seeing at all. But he wisely tried to change the subject.

I, however, still needed to talk. To share my feelings. To let it all out. To find a support group of people who would understand how awful it is to discover a frog the size of a cat in the toilet, half-hidden under the seat.

Now, to be perfectly honest, for years I have chuckled about others who have had such frog shocks. Unsuspecting tourists. Visitors. Year-round residents who think the certificate of occupancy for their new home meant it was frog-proofed.

As much as I have snickered over frogs in coffee cups, cars, thermos bottles and other people's bathrooms, never in my life have I seen a frog quite so calculating, quite so large, quite so ready to

66

attack as this one.

What normal adult is expected to respond quietly, in soft, soothing tones, under these circumstances? I did what every Mature Adult would do. Seeing the glint in its eye, seeing the foam on its mouth and its fangs, I ran backward screaming into the next room. Someone had to alert the world!

No one has ever been able to tell me how frogs of any size get into houses and find their way to plumbing ponds. If it is through screen doors, I have never seen them hopping across the living room in search of kitchen swamplands.

If one frog can make it, what about all his friends? You can't make an exception and keep one as a pet named Kermit. It just won't work, even if you like them. Your house will soon be croaking.

Frogs know that aside from the initial shock of their presence, they will get good mileage out of the aftershocks, so to speak. A large frog, such as MML's, is about a seven on the Creature Fright Scale.

The aftershocks are defined as those occurrences which happen moments or days later, when you are thinking about the original event.

Therefore, I could blame the frog for my subsequent failure to take the right keys with me. And, I have also decided not to clean my bathroom anymore.

"I fail to see the connection," said MML.

"I was cleaning the mirror when you pointed out the frog in your toilet," I said.

"My good deed has created a permanent scar on my psyche. My trust of commodes will never be the same. As a child, I knew a fox inhabited the one nearest the bedroom. Adults said it wasn't true, but they failed to convince me.

"So maybe it wasn't a fox. It was a frog. The surprise is all the same," I said, warming to the subject.

"What would you have done if I hadn't been home?" asked MML.

"I would have called Auburn."

"I fail to see . . ."

"Maybe Youngest Child would be able to come home on an early flight."

"I fail . . ."

"You see, in my single parent years, she was the one I could count on to catch the frogs and put them outside. I paid her handsomely for her trouble. I had to. Sometimes I think she might

67

have brought one or two in just to make some extra money, removing them upon discovery."

I took MML's preoccupation with his magazine as a sign he finally understood.

"So we can go out to eat Saturday night?" I asked.

"If there is a connection, I don't want to know," sighed MML.

The Victim of a Dental Lottery

I learned there had been a "bounty" on my head *after* I was strapped into the dentist chair.

The dental technician (a masked woman who said she knew who my family was and where they lived, and could even identify them by the gold in their mouth) said I had been the topic of a hastily called office meeting.

She said that when the receptionist announced she had convinced me to come in to have my teeth cleaned, everyone dropped the tiny picks and shovels and drills and cheered wildly.

It was then that my dentist threw wet floss on their good cheer with this cautionary note.

"You can't count her until she comes in and sits in the chair," he said.

Mournful silence. Gloom. They all knew how I avoid their place of employment.

It has been two years and five months since my dentist said he wanted me to have my wisdom teeth pulled within 30 days. He made me sit in his chair with cotton in my cheeks until I promised. He didn't see that I had my toes crossed.

My philosophy of dental work is if it doesn't hurt, don't go looking for trouble. My wisdom teeth have never given me a moment's trouble. I like them just fine.

So because I hadn't followed through on my promise since

then, I felt I should not return to my dentist's office for any other reason. Maybe he would forget me. Maybe my file would self-destruct from inactivity at the three year mark.

Maybe not. His telemarketer caught me at a weak moment at work. She noticed it had been awhile since I had been in for teeth cleaning, and just happened to have an opening in ten minutes.

Too soon. She also had one for the next day, and the next. I ran out of excuses.

I was a fugitive patient. On the run, with a posse from the American Dental Society in hot pursuit. I didn't know my dentist had taken a special graduate course in how to convince the skittish patient to return. I am a Mature Adult. I am mostly responsible.

I brush my teeth after eating gummy bears. I have milk products in my diet (even if they are in the form of ice cream bars). I eat apples. I have an average of 10 cavities a decade. I simply choose to have them taken care of at one sitting rather than endure annual trauma or annual repairs.

I figure, given my negative frame of mind toward dental work, that I am actually doing my dentist a favor by *not* coming in more often. I thereby do not cause a ruckus among other patients, perhaps waiting for their first experience in the chair.

He should be thanking me for not demanding monthly dental work.

Of course, now that I recall, his staff did schedule me for lunch time, when no one else was reading magazines in the lobby, and even the receptionist was out, spending the loot she received from my "catch."

I told my masked technician not to bother with X-rays. "Don't find anything wrong," I said.

"I'm not in the mood for drills today," I said.

She did her best, but had to admit reluctantly that all they could see missing was half a filling.

"When would you like to come back to fix it?" she said, offering to write the appointment in the receptionist's calendar.

I used my best ruse. I need to check my schedule back at work, I said.

"I win the bet," the technician yelled. "I said you would say you would call us, not to call you. I win. I win. This is more fun than the lottery . . ."

I slipped out while she was chortling. Half a filling was plenty for that tooth. My wisdom teeth were intact. I had a new tooth

brush for my trouble, gleaming teeth, and a dental floss sample kit which I gave to a child for kite string.
    Safe for another two years.

Life in a Petting Zoo

No matter what room we enter, we are followed by a petting zoo. The threesome is underfoot at every step.

Petting Zoo is comprised of our two old canines, and Fluffy.

The moment either of us stands up or moves in the direction of the kitchen, Fluffy has one thought on her mind: food. Of course, MML has also been spoiling her with new treats — smelly, oily, canned cat food, which she dearly loves now that she has tasted it.

So any trip to the kitchen rings the cat food-bell in her mind. And we suffer the consequences of such coddling. Fluffy weaves her body between our feet at every step just to remind us that there is a hungry cat also headed for the refrigerator. It does not matter to her that she has just eaten. She would gladly trip the hand that feeds her for the chance to eat that fishy stuff again.

The minute the Dog Boys see Fluffy lobbying for more, they join her in the race for anything edible.

I am embarrassed to report that the net result has not improved my image as a less-than-graceful person, as I stumble through the Petting Zoo to answer the kitchen phone. And members of this gang of three are equally protective of their petting rights.

If Fluffy jumps into a lap, Dog Boys appear immediately to have their ears scratched.

If the Boys want in or out, so does Fluffy. I am thinking of taking them all for group therapy, to deal with their jealousy issues. The Boys have even quarreled over Fluffy's affections. It was not a pretty sight. My Dog feels that Fluffy is his cat because they have lived together for so many years.

Other Dog seems to feel that as long as the cat is fickle, he has a chance. Personally, I think it has more to do with wanting what Fluffy has in her bowl, than it does actually caring for the cat herself. The moment she is done, and sometimes even sooner, the dogs vie to make sure that Fluffy has not left so much as a morsel behind.

Efforts to reduce the zoo's population have met with resistance from those one would think would be delighted to permanently entertain an old dog.

As I planned a recent trip north by car, I asked my son if there was anything I could bring him in Washington.

"Nothing that is 45 pounds of lumps and black fur," he said.

So much for dropping off The Dog, his dog, in the nation's capital.

I was no more successful in my attempt to place Fluffy Up North with Middle Child.

She said Fluffy would not get along with her new kitten.

I ask you, is that my problem? Should I lose sleep over potential animal relationships in a northern state?

No, I've got enough problems trying to walk from my chair to the kitchen without stumbling over someone furry.

About the only place Fluffy doesn't dog our heels, so to speak, is on our walks about town.

It may be laziness on her part, or she may realize that she would risk becoming entangled in the leashes. The dogs manage to make themselves as underfoot on a walk as they do in the house.

They twist their leashes into a maypole at least once in the course of every walk, and head in opposite directions. Then, having set us off balance, they move directly into our path.

We, who are trying to provide a comfortable and loving home for these old fellows in their golden years, wind up looking mighty foolish as we walk the brick streets.

Now that the children have apartments of their own, shouldn't they take responsibility for their pets? Should I take their "no's" for an answer?

Or should I just count my blessings that it is just two old dogs and a cat that comprise our *menagerie à trois* — that the children did not leave me with pets that multiply, like rabbits?

Time Release Calories

Sometime in the last few months, I have inadvertently ingested time-release calories.

They may have been hidden in Christmas cookies or wedding cake, or I might have eaten them during a trip north last fall.

I know I have them because, as I start on week one of my new diet, I am gaining weight. It is not so much that I weigh more than when I began my latest efforts to return to the basic size of most of my wardrobe. Rather, I am not losing. To my way of thinking, if I am not showing a significant decrease when I step on my scales (after all my careful efforts at the table) then indeed I am gaining, and my dietary efforts are merely holding back the tide.

Dry toast. Grapefruit. Cottage cheese. An apple. Vegetables. Diet sodas. No cookies. No crackers. No cheese. No good stuff.

That's what I mean. I've been behaving for a week, and have *more* to show for it than I care to.

I didn't have cinnamon buns at a downtown festival.

All right, I didn't stay totally on my diet at that event. I had a grilled sausage, a spicy crab cake and a homemade pretzel. That was all. Should I gain a half-pound because of that, with all the walking back and forth we did?

Well, okay. I did have half a submarine sandwich at noon, but that was because we had company from out of town and had to serve something. Doesn't it count that I didn't eat more than one cookie after lunch?

And shouldn't the half-mile walk from my house to the bridge help abate the effects of the caloric intake? I should think so.

That is why I am convinced that science has not studied enough about when calories will strike.

They say that the tendency toward certain diseases is established in childhood — the way we were fed and how much sun we got.

So why not calories as well? As a kid I was skinny. They called me "Bag of Bones Bailey." I could and did eat anything. Especially at picnics.

So now, in my middle age, those childhood hamburger and potato chip calories have found me at last, along with those

75

implanted in Man in My Life's recipe for his mother's oatmeal cookies. It is sort of like having a long-term bond mature.

I realize the time has come to be responsible. I would like to blame someone for my current dilemma. I would like to blame MML for making those cookies during a six-week period just before Christmas. But being a responsible, Mature Adult, I must hold myself at fault for eating them. Lots of them and peanut butter cookies as well, which I baked.

Besides, if I blame him, then he won't bake me more once I have successfully completed my diet regime.

Maybe I shouldn't go to any more town events. But that would be shirking my civic duty. Local organizations rely on the proceeds from their savory food booths to continue their worthy projects the rest of the year.

Maybe I'll look for the tent where cottage cheese and dry toast is sold. If it is sold out, oh well. I'll have no choice but to support the other concessions.

Getting Double Duty
From the Tree

I just discovered my grapefruit tree isn't.

It had been so long since I planted it and another small citrus tree in my back yard that I had forgotten their names. Because neither had borne fruit in the past eight years or so since I had set them free from life in a pot, their identities became confused.

Now, just as I am planning additions to my house and am making decisions about which plants will be moved, the "grapefruit" tree sent forth seven fruit. They seemed small, but I figured for a first effort, at least they were worth harvesting.

Unsure of when these fruit should be picked, I left them on the tree. But as I glanced at my crop just a few days ago, I first thought that it had "gone by," a northern term I have learned from my husband. It means gone past its prime.

The color was distinctively orange. My grapefruit, joy of joys, are tangelos — my favorite fruit. So the hired woodsman will be asked to spare that tree.

I know that people who study these things can tell the difference between varieties of citrus. I can't. After nearly 12 years in Florida I am able to distinguish between some flora — pineapples and coconuts, for example. And between hibiscus and gerbera daisies. That's as far as it goes.

My early training in botanical things was Up North where we had violets and daffodils and maples and everyone could clearly see what was what. Weeds were weeds, not some exotic tropical plant which if left alone, would perfume the neighborhood.

It was a land where Christmas trees smelled like they should and cost less than the sum total of Christmas presents for the entire family.

When I discovered in 1978 that it would take the better part of a week's paycheck to buy an "imported Up North pine," I purchased a realistic artificial tree, which I figured would pay for itself after a few years.

"But it doesn't smell right," said the children.

"And its needles aren't falling. It isn't any fun," they said, booking their airline flight back to New York for the holidays.

"But these prices are outrageous," I said, year after year.

"We had 8-feet-high and 6-feet-wide trees up north for one-dollar-a-foot. I could buy us all a new wardrobe for the cost of a tree like that down here," I noted.

They were still packing.

"Tell you what, no more artificial. I'll get a real tree," I said, some years ago.

But I couldn't bring myself to pay $30 at the Up North tree stand by the Banana House.

I stopped at the garden center and bought something in a pot I could plant later.

"Mom, our presents look stupid under a grapefruit tree," said my critics.

My subsequent efforts with various small, potted pines have met with similar dismay.

"But look how ecological this is. We are now on the Audubon Society's Christmas list for recycling our tree into back yard landscaping," I said.

"No deal," said the children.

"We want a real tree."

So this year, in anticipation of their return for the holidays, I purchased a "real" tree. It is real small, to fit my budget. And it looks nice, to my way of thinking — with all the traditional family decorations. It has the popsicle stick ornament my son made when he was in first grade, a paper angel ornament (with her photograph on it) that Youngest Child fashioned at some point, and French horns from Middle Child.

It has everything that a large tree would hold, in a compact area.

"Tree clutter," said Man in My Life. He prefers — how shall I say this carefully — a more organized approach to the tree (an artificial one at that) than I am prone to take.

He also knows what kinds of citrus trees he has in his yard.

Given our basic differences in decoration, I suspect when we have a combined household, we will end up with two Christmas trees.

There will be one carefully adorned with just the right amount of garlands and ornaments — one with all the strands of lights working. And its needles won't drop and it won't need watering.

And in my private work area, among the other clutter and

disarray, will be the second — small, live and covered with everything. All the seasonal mementos. And when I put away the tinsel in January, I'll eat the grapefruit before I plant it.

Paneful Lessons

I promise to never make fun of helpless animals again. Promise.

My elderly step-dog (who has yet to learn a trick) does not have a reputation for being the brains among our pet family. He has other redeeming qualities that his true owner, my new husband, does not see as readily as I do. For example, his dog has soft ears.

But I confess to blurting out a guffaw when I saw Rascal walking head first into the sliding glass doors at our new house. There was a terrible thud just before my laugh. I wasn't kind, and I plan to do community service at the wildlife center for my lack of sensitivity.

That was before Saturday morning when I headed in the dark for the kitchen to get coffee. There was a terrible thudding noise. I had walked into the same doors. At that hour, I failed to see the humor of such poetic justice.

I'm wondering if wandering into glass has something to do with our new neighborhood. I have lived in Southwest Florida for years, have had many sliding glass doors to navigate, and normally have had someone competent at my helm.

And, as far as I know, the dogs have not suffered such humiliating experiences either, until now.

The reason I am wondering if it has something to do with our move is because of a question our neighbor posed the other night.

"Has the cardinal been at your house?" she asked.

While we have not had much time for birdwatching, we had to admit that the cardinal we had seen fluttering about next-door

79

among the pines had not shown much interest in our arrival. We thought it might be the presence of Fluffy, although she has chosen to stay indoors since the move.

Our neighbor said that the cardinal, for two years, has been flying from the pine trees into the glass windows on their porch. For two years. All day long.

They figured the bird had built up unusual neck muscles by this time. But this week, they heard an especially loud thud against the pane.

My neighbor went out, and there was the cardinal, belly-up on the lawn — its eyes glazed; its breathing labored.

Periodically, she checked on the bird, stroking its little feathered head. After several hours the cardinal came to and resumed his "paneful" obsession.

"Would you like to borrow Fluffy?" I asked helpfully.

"She's old and hasn't caught anything since her 10th birthday, but your skydiver might not know the difference if we tie her to the pine tree for awhile."

My neighbor said she was used to the thudding, which starts as soon as the bird wakes up at dawn.

I didn't think Fluffy would really harm the mad bomber from the Wild Kingdom. I just envisioned her as part of an animal neighborhood watch which might help scare the nuisance away.

But Fluffy won't go outside anymore, so it is a moot issue.

At my other house, she was banished to the outdoors in 1982 when Youngest Child developed terrible cat allergies.

Then after the children left home, I let Fluffy continue to live in nature, primarily because I didn't want to trip over her every time I walked to the kitchen. And most important, I did not want her to sleep on my face in the middle of the night.

Man in My Life likes cats. He likes Fluffy. He felt sorry for her. After we were married, he began acquiring little things which should have warned me of his intentions — a litter box, for example.

Cats that live outside don't need them. I should have known.

During the move itself, we decided to leave the cat at my house for a few days. We stopped by to feed her and visit with her, but I was afraid that if we brought her with us, she would escape before she was acclimated to our new house, and it would be good-bye, old cat.

Ha. MML and Fluffy had it all planned.

He had her box ready, and extra little treats to make her

feel welcome.

Curiosity lured the cat to leave the house for 15 minutes on Saturday to see what was in the garage. She went as far as its edge, probably where the head-banging cardinal was in full view, and ran back in the house. I can not talk her into stepping through that door again.

And recent company spoiled her further until, feeling completely secure and kittenish, she hopped onto their bed, purred too loudly, hogged the sheets and nibbled toes.

Thud. Fluffy found herself out in the hall with the guest room door firmly closed.

Perhaps we have all learned our lessons. Fluffy promises to show more restraint with company; Rascal and I will be more careful with doors, and I also plan to purchase a bunch of colorful decals for the sliders — some at dog's eye level, and some at mine.

I'd offer to get my neighbors some cat decals for their lanai windows, but I'm afraid that their red bird might get spooked in our direction.

Spikey, Call Home

Somewhere, lost in the sub-tropical foliage of downtown, is Spikey.

The reward poster, plastered on power poles, tells the story. The owner says Spikey is friendly. Just because he is a three-foot iguana doesn't mean he bites.

Spikey seems to be cold-blooded about his family's feelings. They have provided a loving home and are concerned enough to offer a reward for his return. Lizards are not furry enough for me. The closest I have come to owning a pet from the reptile family is a turtle.

We had a pet turtle, dime store variety, when my son was a baby. Our Chicago apartment did not allow anything with fur or feathers, so we settled on a turtle. The turtle met a terrible end, I'm sad to report. Its little dish was on top of the radiator, which we later learned, was controlled by a central maintenance system.

The weather was still warm; our windows were open. It never dawned on us that the janitor's schedule to turn on the heat had nothing to do with the outside temperature. We sadly learned that turtles do not fare well in hot tubs.

Being an animal lover, I have been keeping my eye out for Spikey, and say to myself as I take my daily bicycle ride, "If I were an iguana, where would I be hiding?"

It's not the $25 reward that has me looking. In truth, I would not stop and coax him into my bicycle basket so we could ride to the nearest poster for the owner's phone number.

I would rather not be the rescuer. I would just like to see him safely back in his pen so that he does not surprise me in the back yard some morning—sitting there sunning himself and ballooning his throat with the small lizards.

Our family has had its share of exotic pets, and ordinary ones as well. Fortunately, none of the children wanted snakes or lizards. They did have mice once or twice, birds, hamsters, guinea pigs, ducks (several small flocks), numerous dogs and cats, and rabbits.

Most of the time, as a mother who was always trying to make everybody happy, I would let them get a pet to cheer them up when something sad happened. There is nothing like a puppy or chinchilla to brighten a day.

The first year after the divorce, we had to apply for a zoo license. You get the picture.

However, on one occasion, we acquired a rabbit by other means.

For mystical reasons, Youngest Child was selected for many years to be "the person from the audience," any audience, to assist performers with their acts.

At Busch Gardens, she was chosen to help with the bird show. At Sea World, she was chosen to feed something that was swimming.

At the county auditorium, she was chosen by Blackstone the Magician from a capacity crowd, from the back of the audience, to help him with his rabbit act.

She was seven. She wanted to keep the rabbit after he pulled it from her hat.

Surprised, Blackstone gave it to her. It was also very young. She named it "Peru."

Peru was not only young, he was not in good health. Or he was unaccustomed to living outside a hat. In any case, the rabbit only lived a day or so, breaking my child's heart.

"Don't cry," said I, the emotional fix-it mother.

"Would you like another bunny, puppy, or ducks? I'd get you a pony, but the county zoning people would say 'no.' "

She was inconsolable.

"How about two kittens and a canary?"

"I want Peru stuffed," she sobbed.

I hate to admit this, but I actually looked into it. I learned the cost of immortalizing Peru was considerably steeper than my subsequent trip to the animal family burial plot.

And to make her feel better, we settled on a kitten named Gonzo, who was willing to have his teeth brushed and didn't seem to mind wearing doll dresses.

He didn't run away either. Not like the large lizard on the prowl in my city.

My heart goes out to Spikey's owners. They even might have a small child who has enjoyed dressing this pet and taking him for rides in a doll buggy. It is a bad time of year, the holidays, for pets to wander.

Spikey, call home.

The Wild Wild West

There were several things wrong with my horse. I was looking for something slow and dependable to take me up the Colorado mountain in my recent discovery of the Wild West.

It didn't matter that Rocket made his living following the tail of his stablemates through the sagebrush and aspen. I hadn't seen his credentials before I put my foot in the stirrup and no one seemed to know the contents of his resumé.

"How many of you are advanced riders?" asked the cowgirl. All but my hand went up. I wasn't about to admit that I had riding lessons as a child and had even jumped 4-foot fences in horse shows. Too many years have gone by.

Our trail leader might expect me to survive a trot.

As one of the "beginners," I had a lesson in how to hold the reins and was provided with useful information on what to do in case of an avalanche, holdup, roundup or rattlesnake ambush. Unfortunately I missed the details because Rocket wanted to eat something green. Our leader said not to let the horses eat. I decided that one little bit wouldn't hurt especially if I wanted to make a friend of my mount before we started on the dusty trail.

But there are deficiencies in the design of the horse. Where was the glove compartment? There was no place to put my new disc camera except to loop its strap around the saddle horn.

That worked fine until Rocket launched into his first quick trot, DOWN a steep slope. My camera, bouncing with each step, took six pictures of my knee.

During the trot I looked for the brakes. I even pedaled backward. However, Rocket seemed to be missing some of the extras featured on later models. There was no second gear for hills, and my steed had a compulsion for conformity equaled only by lemmings.

He wanted to keep up with the horse ahead, no matter what direction perpendicular to the horizon we were traveling.

And frankly, I missed the reclining bucket seats. Our trail boss suggested that to help the horses keep their balance, we (the surviving riders) should lean forward going up hill, and lean way back going down. Unfortunately I soon found that the saddles were not constructed for this bit of gymnastic activity.

And where was the steering control? It was misplaced in the horse's mouth. I have new respect for Roy Rogers and what he must have endured on the trail.

Whoever designed horses did not take into consideration their frequent need for fuel and emission control. I suspect some federal regulations are needed to set some uniform standards on the American models if we are to discourage imports.

Don't ask me about horsepower. Rocket needed a tuneup if anyone had plans to enter him in a derby, but I didn't want to see him attempt any greater burst of speed than he exhibited at the top of the ridge.

"Isn't this fun?" said the dean of a Western university on a large horse ahead of me. "I think I'll buy a horse when I get home," she said.

I'm in no rush. I think I'll wait to see if the fall models include enclosed seating areas and an FM radio.

A Stream of Thoughts on Rain

Caution: If you are trying to persuade friends or family members to move to sunny Southwest Florida, don't send them this book. They may not want to buy the lot next to yours, and I can't be responsible for the loss of a sale.

The excessive rain is making me cranky. Besides being in flood denial where my own house is concerned (located on the banks of a swollen canal, four blocks from the cresting river), my doors are swollen shut, my stamps are stuck to each other, my rugs feel like sponges and every envelope in the house needs to be steamed open before use. My drip-dry clothes don't.

And to top it off, my umbrellas are as wet on the inside as on the outside.

I never learned proper techniques for using them in heavy

downpours. They are useful but clumsy inventions which need new design features for southern torrents. I don't even know if there are instructions for this kind of deluge. By the time I fold my umbrella and get in my car, I am as wet as if I hadn't used one.

Bah, humbug. So this is the sunny South. I moved here to get away from weather. Up North we had snow and more snow, and light rain the rest of the year. I had my glasses tinted as I left so that I could gradually adjust to the bright light of Florida.

The recent bad weather has its own bright side. I sold my back yard last week to people from Michigan who wanted swamp land while it was still on the market.

They were rowing down my street at 5 p.m. They heard that swamps were being paved over by malls, and this last vestige of real Florida would no longer be available.

I said I had a deal for them, if they would take it off my hands before its waters encroached on my bedroom floor.

I'm trying to be positive and upbeat. So my positive thought is this. Those working on city improvements may be able to capitalize on the flooding as a unique natural water attraction: street-swimming. My children used to love to do it on Marion Avenue by the Methodist Church.

I thought my children were in the house watching television during the No Name Storm. I called from work to get an update on whether the rising river could be seen yet from the house. No answer.

Repeated calls. No answer. Maybe they were bobbing frantically in the living room, trying to reach the phone as it swirled past them among the flotsam that was once our precious clutter. Maybe the youngest was being rescued by our hero dog. Perhaps she was clinging to his furry neck and he was paddling her to high ground formerly known as the kitchen table.

Maybe not.

Neighbors said they saw all three street-swimming with The Dog. Later the kids happily reported that they saw fish and snakes navigating the brick streets.

Surely there was an ordinance against swimming in a church zone. Why hadn't someone sent a lifeguard?

Up North, rain is mostly steady drizzle, except when we went camping in the woods — then it was full-faucet weekend. But good Northerners are prepared. We had fluorescent rain gear with hoods, and boots and large black umbrellas. And when drizzle got cold and turned to sleet and snow, we were prepared. We had mittens and boots and heavy jackets and hats.

Boots. I haven't seen a boot, except cowboy boots, since I moved to Florida. An entrepreneur with an amphibious aircraft could have made a killing on any street in this area with a floating concession stand for rubber boots.

It has been many years since I thought of the advantages of snow. But under the present circumstances, I will share one that came to mind in the last squall.

When the snow gets deep you can move it out of your way with a shovel. That is not a property of excessive rain. I have seen no rain shovels in local stores, though I would like to move the water from my yard. I am ready to see if any of the children are ready to let their mother move in their Northern apartments with them.

I recognize that my attitude may mean a visit from the "enlightenment" committee of the Chamber of Commerce, but they'll need to get their wading boots to make a house call.

Beyond Chicken Soup

There isn't enough vitamin C left on citrus trees here in May to cure me.

Somewhere along the line I picked up the wrong kind of cold, but don't know where to exchange it.

It was designed last January for a 4-year-old — a pre-schooler whose mother won the National Chicken Soup contest three years in a row.

My cold was wrongly delivered on May 12 during my mini-vacation on Sanibel. Besides hourly soup, it calls for the following treatment: a comforter and a poultice of Vicks, buckets of fresh orange juice, warm bunny slippers and a coloring book.

This child's cold has already boosted the stock market's index for tissues.

My cold is not a working-person-in-southwest-Florida's cold. Nor was it the kind of cold you would invite on a beach holiday if you had a choice. The Southwest Florida adult cold would have responded to fresh air and sunshine and heat. It would have been gone after a few hours of Gulf breezes and biking. It might even have had the consideration to post some warning signs during the weekend then wait until Monday to hit me.

Instead, this child's cold demanded freezing, snowy weather and sweaters and lots of pillows and toys to play with indoors.

No one should feel feverish when it is already 90 degrees outside.

When I have had a few other rare colds, I have known where they've come from. I am usually the last person at the office to get sick, just as sympathy has run out for the first few victims and the survivors have returned to work. They have forgotten how rotten they felt a week earlier. I am on my own with the last cold at work.

This time around, I actually may be the first to have something first — the one to start the cold front.

On the other hand, this is not an adult cold. My co-workers might be safe.

It is the kind of cold a child could tell the truth about and still stay home from school.

That is a heartless comment from a mother of three, but it comes from practical experience. My youngest child was, shall I say, a bit prone to hypochondria. She liked missing a day of school now and then to watch television.

Her ruses became increasingly devious, so I wanted proof of severe illness before I would give in. The fever had to be certifiably raging; stomach flu evident; X-rays confirmed.

One of her creative efforts included heating her thermometer in her cup of chicken noodle soup. The plan failed as the mercury soared and popped the end off her thermometer, prompting some well-deserved maternal questions.

With her track record for invented morning illnesses, sneezing just wasn't enough for me to let the youngest child miss school. Then came The Day She Really Was Sick. She sneezed for two weeks and finally claimed she was too weak to go to school. That pushed her credibility to the limit. To call her bluff, I took her to the doctor. The youngest sat down on the elevator floor.

"Get up," I hissed. "You're creating a scene."

"I can't stand. We'll see who's right. You never believe me," she said.

"This child could get an Oscar for her 'My Stomach Hurts On Test Days,'" I told the other elevator passengers as I smiled confidently.

The doctor confirmed the diagnosis. Youngest Child's. Indeed, she had pneumonia and immediate admission papers to the hospital — all from sneezing.

She has never let me live it down. So I learned my lesson. Even hypochondriacs get sick.

I am not one of them, though. I have a cold. I am a middle-aged person in Florida, in mid-May with a craving for hot cocoa, a Teddy bear, milk toast and quilts, even though it is 89 degrees at supper time.

And I wish someone would write a note that says I don't have to go to school tomorrow. Otherwise, help me find the kid that this cold belongs to.

Don't Send the Cat

My plans to wrap Fluffy in a brown paper bundle and deposit her with appropriate postage at the Post Office are on temporary hold.

My middle child says "no."

She is moving into new housing on the first of March. It is a place which allows pets. She never should have told me that.

I was moderately interested in the fact that it is an historic home, and that she and her roommate are taking on a third companion to help share the cost. I am tolerant and trusting about the fact that the third companion is a male. (We all watched *Three's Company* long enough to see how well that situation can work.)

I was mildly interested in how nice the floors sounded and in the apartment's location near the middle child's art school.

But what caused me to spill my coffee was her news that the

landlord allowed pets.

"Fluffy is on her way," I said.

I have waited patiently through Abbie's four years of college for that news from Up North because she has inquired weekly about the state of health of her elderly pet.

This is her old pal. The cat who used to sleep with her. The cat she sits with and feeds tidbits and little drinks of milk when she is home for a visit.

This is the cat she wants to know if I am petting on a regular basis.

This is the cat who is always looking for the middle child. Always.

But, suddenly, the voice from Up North is not very interested. I detect an underlying lust for a kitten, not an old cat. She would deny that, of course. Her excuse is that the trip would be too hard on her pet.

"Fluffy loved her three-day ride from New York 10 years ago with you kids and the dog. Just because she escaped in Atlanta does not mean she wasn't having a wonderful time playing the alphabet game," I said.

"Fluffy is so old," said my daughter. "What if her heart gave out on the plane? She has really made a wonderful adjustment to Florida after all these years, Mom. And, besides, she would miss The Dog, and there aren't any lizards to chase up here in the snow."

"Ah, her coat is an Up North variety," I replied. "She doesn't move six months of the year."

"She's used to it now. She's retired," said the girl I thought I knew.

It is true. Fluffy has finally adjusted well to life in Florida. Better than I had expected. She sits by the back door and watches the exotic wildlife feed from her cat dish. I know because I have seen her late night dinner parties with possums and raccoons.

Frankly, I don't like Middle Child's attitude. College learning has gone to her head. Now, I don't think I want Fluffy to go north after all. I'm not sure she could cope with public transportation and seaport life and cobble streets.

Even if Middle Child begs, this cat is staying here.

She has her nerve wanting to take Fluffy away from the home *my* cat has come to love. I suppose next she, or her brother or sister will want The Dog. Just let them try to talk me into giving up the old dirty-laundry-snatcher himself.

Drumming Up
Childhood Memories

Although my son is not quite 25, I fear he is entering his second childhood. He was always advanced for his age, so I should have anticipated that he would have another go at his formative years quite early in life.

He called me from Washington the other day to say, among other things, that he was constructing a drum set.

A friend is helping him with it. Whatever they are making it out of escapes me, but I'm sure it will be noisy.

The news gave me a *déjà vu* headache. You see, 20 years ago he talked a doting grandparent into buying him a drum set for Christmas. He carefully circled his first choice in the discount catalogue, calculated the sales tax (which doting grandparents always found cute), and said it was the only thing he wanted as a present that year.

The set, now on a list of banned toys (established by a militant national group called Mothers Against Noise), came complete with a snare drum, a trap drum, a bass drum, cymbals, a cowbell, drum sticks and a pedal for the big drum.

It was made of durable space-age materials, of course. Virtually indestructible, as the ad explained. It could be dropped off Pike's Peak and sustain no damage. Maybe such an experiment would not break the drums, but it might have taken him a few days to find them again.

As a childhood set, there was no chance of it wearing out in the first hour, month or year of abuse by small boys, or through the sudden violent reaction of a mother who had had enough.

It was the deluxe model, made to last.

His grandmother lived in another city, so the full impact of her gift was never understood, even when I had to shout over the beat to talk with her on the phone.

My boy, and his friend Jimmy, soon discovered the Monkees, a post-Beatles singing group. I can remember their theme song, sung over and over by two 5-year-olds, who were still fond of the same lyrics at 6 and 7.

"Hey, hey we're the Monkees, and people say we monkey around . . ."

I did my best not to be an interfering mother. I hid in remote corners of the house while they practiced for a future career in show biz. But because of their need for an audience every 15 minutes or so, the drums had a way of finding me, no matter where I was.

It was during some grand roll-off years later that the pedal punctured the bass drum, and the set was doomed. I was ready to help carry it to the curb or bury it in the back yard, whichever the boys would allow.

Instead, Christopher, understanding marketing principles, turned this "threat" into "opportunity" and sold the tattered set to his younger sister.

It became the first of several similar deals to his trusting sibling.

He also sweet-talked her into purchasing a large piece of black velvet (which he borrowed back as needed for film backdrops) and a broken train set.

She put the drums in her closet. I wish I had thought to give her front money to hide them sooner.

I should have suspected that his love affair with percussion was not over when he began to ask for bits and pieces of noisy things for Christmas and birthdays during college. The symptoms should have been obvious. A starving undergraduate does not ask for a wood block and *real* cowbells if he is not trying to return to his youth.

I should have known when he asked if I remembered Jimmy's last name and whether or not he still had a cymbal set.

I guess I was figuring that children had to wait their turn — that I was entitled to a second childhood before he began his. And so I ignored all the signs, even when he began watching reruns of *Sesame Street.*

Now, some Washington, D.C. neighborhood — not his mother's — is going to be lucky to hear the drums of Chris and Jimmy. And it is just as well. Their windows are likely to be tightly closed most of the year. Ours are not.

But just in case the audience is not enthusiastic when the weather is warmer, I think I'll warn his sister in Boston to hold on to her money when this new set of drums comes on the market — unless he is willing to trade back the piece of black velvet and broken train set as part of the deal.

A Bite Taken Out of Summer Fun

For at least five minutes each summer, I wonder if I made the right decision.

It occurs to me that when I lived Up North, hot was 80 degrees, humidity was defined as the mist from a lawn sprinkler, and, to the best of my recollection, there were no fleas and few mosquitoes.

Admittedly, the tip of Long Island, where I spent many childhood summers, had nasty insects. The four mosquitoes assigned to our cottage made up for their lack of numbers with the severity of their bites and the itchiness they caused. The effects of a good nip on one's legs lasted all of July. We had bright pink spots of Calamine lotion covering 85 percent of our bodies and scars to show that we had not listened to our parents' admonitions not to scratch where we had been bitten.

This year the mosquitoes are as bad as I can remember in the 11 years since I headed south with three children, a dog and a cat.

The mosquitoes are joined by clouds of (I fear) carnivorous fruit flies which hover over my rotting mango crop in the yard. And they have marshalled an auxiliary force of fleas which took over the Dog Boys in May during the dry season.

The rains did not dampen the spirits of the fleas, as promised by an optimist who has no pets.

But the worst byproduct of the rains were the mosquitoes and the pungent decay of my unwanted fruit crop.

The problem isn't only in my yard, however. Bugs are bad all over Southwest Florida. I read recently that it is not a good idea to stick your arm out the car window. A mosquito count by experts shows one arm instantly attracts hundreds of mosquitoes. The numbers which can be found on a bare arm in less than a minute are astronomical. I am not volunteering for the count. One mosquito lighting would be sufficient.

"Drive on," I would tell the official counter. "I've seen enough to satisfy me that we should call for mosquito control."

I have no intention of doing that, nor do I want to put my arm out of the door of my house these days.

Letting the dogs back in is trick enough. Their black coats provide camouflage for the winged assailants who have me as their target. The fruit flies join them, purely on speculation. Their feast is outdoors, but they may be tired of the mango fare, as am I.

Dragonflies, which reportedly prey on mosquitoes, have been detained this year. No other natural predators have come forth in my neighborhood to tackle the insect invasion.

My repellents seem inadequate to the task. I'm wondering if anyone makes mosquito collars or dip for people.

On a recent trip to the Okefenokee Swamp, what was left of my mosquito-bitten limbs was attacked by yellow flies.

At first I thought the commercial repellent sold at the tourist stand was providing the shield I needed while everyone else was dancing and slapping themselves on the nature trails.

But I learned something about yellow-fly bites. They don't itch for two days. They swell into lumps and send out strong signals that they need violent scratching. One good scratch on the finger sets off a bite behind the knee, and so forth.

At least our local mosquito does not cause a long-lasting itch. It doesn't need to. It has the fleas and fire ants to provide residual discomfort.

My five minutes of wishing-I-were-back-North are up.

I'll go back to cheerfully coping with the elements, and plan an indoor picnic for my friends.

94

Crunchy Stuffing

My children will be home for Thanksgiving. It will be the first time the gang has assembled at the homestead in as long as anyone can remember.

To mark the occasion, I will have a large bird on the table. It is a Gemini Feast Day — one that those of us born in May choose to spend our cooking time on.

I look forward to Thanksgiving and to having my offspring watch the parade, offer to help set the table, serve and do dishes. They never did that before, but they were younger then. I'm sure that without prompting, looking after their mother will come naturally. To show her the honor she is due as head of the household.

So it did not come as a surprise that my son would offer, long distance, to fix the turkey.

"No," I said. "The turkey is mine. I have you down for gravy."

"No," he said, "You don't understand. We don't like the way you do it."

"No?" I said. "Since when do you dare criticize the hand that paid for plane tickets to Florida."

"We've all talked it over," he said. "We don't like your stuffing. It's crunchy."

"That's the way wild rice is supposed to be," I said.

"We want mushy bread dressing just like grandma used to make."

"Then maybe you should go over the river and through the woods. My bird always is stuffed with rice and mushrooms."

"Actually, it was the crunchy mushrooms we didn't care for," said my boy. (Obviously he had been elected spokesperson during an earlier three-city family conference call.)

My children were taking advantage of a mother's intense desire to spend a holiday with her children. They would probably stop at nothing now that I tipped my hand and sent them all tickets. Someone would want chocolate cake rather than pumpkin pie. Someone would want macaroni and cheese out of a box rather than sweet potatoes. Someone else would prefer that the salad have optional onions, and they all might vote against turnips appearing within 500 feet of the table. And what if two cans of black olives are not enough? What if someone wants more?

There were other issues. Someone would probably want to sunbathe all day and have leftovers after dark. And could they be trusted *not* to teach The Dog new tricks, especially with wild rice and mushrooms as bait? I didn't like the sound of this at all.

Fear has begun to replace my irrational maternal instincts to welcome them without signed contracts at the airport.

The written legal agreements would specify that their mother is in charge, even if they are bigger than she is. That they will be respectful in front of her friends and not tell their favorite family stories just to get even for what she has been writing about them. That they will appreciate Thanksgiving dinner and the stuffing even if it kills them. That they will help with the dishes, not borrow her new car, be grateful for their personal use of the washer and dryer without charge and leave the homesite as clean as they found it.

For all of this, they may make local calls, walk the dog and bathe him, and buy new toothbrushes in any color they want.

And, if I have such cooperation pledged in writing, they may take turns sitting by the window and going with me to the store. And for good behavior, I will throw in a side dish of that mushy bread stuffing.

"Jumbo" Obstacles on the
Road to Dieting

"Jumbo."

The sad voice next to me on the bench is telling me what he would have preferred to order.

He is looking at an empty frozen yogurt cup. It was the small size. Coconut.

He ordered "small" for both of us because we are on diets. What he really wanted was "jumbo."

I was glad to have a taste of anything sweet, so even "small" was wonderful. But "small" was not enough for Man in My Life. "Jumbo" might have been.

We have become experts on diet treats, planning entire evenings around stressful decisions at the popsicle display in our favorite supermarket.

We have found frozen calories on a stick ranging from 16 to 60, and indulge ourselves depending on how the scales have viewed our daily progress.

Actually, MML could probably have ordered "jumbo." He is doing quite well on his diet, thank you. He is ready to make a trip to the tailor to have his new slacks taken in.

My progress is more in the "medium" category. I am pleased that I no longer need to keep an appointment with an alteration specialist since I have lost enough to get back into some nice outfits that I thought were headed for the church rummage sale.

It is not easy to be a dieter in this little town. Temptations and corruptions are everywhere, at unexpected hours. I have discovered that the road to bulges is paved with red brick. Who would have guessed that at 6:30 a.m. in the waterfront park, a restaurant and a radio station would conspire to seduce dieters who were out exercising?

They set up a booth and handed out free coffee and doughnuts to joggers and bikers. MML jogged on by. I stopped. I barely resisted the call of jelly-filled confections, but learned that it is possible to drink coffee and ride a bike, even on a brick street.

What will they think of next? Will they set up a table and hand out jumbo yogurt cones — bran and blueberry flavored for the pre-breakfast fitness set?

MML resisted the crullers, but I can't expect him, in his present frame of mind, to run by the 90 calorie Georgia peach waffle cone.

We have truly tried to be sensible in this diet. We have acknowledged that as Mature Adults, we need a break from the totally strict regimen, once our bodies learned we were serious about reducing.

We have agreed to having minor treats on special occasions, and are finding many special occasions to celebrate.

It is the mark of maturity to be reasonable. So there was the night we rode bikes to the grocery store to buy diet pop . . . and ginger cookies. My theory is that the bike ride created a negative caloric balance which could then be offset by just one cookie. A longer ride might have justified two, or one and a popsicle.

But those are conscious decisions, to get on bikes and exercise for a diet reward. We know our limits.

It is the unexpected lemonade stand, the surprise of free coffee and doughnuts which makes it difficult to follow the straight and narrow. And being a compassionate, tenderhearted person, I find it very hard to live with the disappointment in MML's voice when his yogurt cup is prematurely empty.

Maybe we can create a new jumbo exercise route — bike around town twice before we stop at the store for our extra large treat.

Maybe it would be less complicated to drive there and bike extra tomorrow.

Yogurt is supposed to be good for us. Maybe we can substitute a "jumbo" for the main course of supper — it will all balance out calorically.

Give me a day or two and I'll have this all figured out.

Taking the Clutter Cure

I have taken the clutter cure. I will not clutter. I will not clutter. I will not clutter or save everything any more. I have seen the light.

It is still a struggle to say those words out loud. But I am well on the way of fighting the family curse of retaining everything.

All these years I thought I was the black sheep of the family. I thought my collections of important *insignificantia* were mine alone, and that my parents maintained a neat and orderly living room free of newspapers and children's lunch boxes or art.

They did. It was all out of sight, squirreled away in the garage and closets. That I did not learn until we, my sisters and I, were responsible for estate matters.

We looked recently at what we think was the last generational clutter. It was a storage shed filled with garage items. Unmarked boxes from the past. I'm cured.

Item: Every letter anyone ever sent anyone.

I don't mean just every letter *I* wrote home from camp at age nine. I mean every letter my mother wrote to her mother, and all the letters my grandmother wrote to her mother, and my paternal grandmother to my father in college and his letters home (all about the weather), and my paternal grandfather's courtship notes to my grandmother (they were interesting).

Resolve: Throw out the old letters I have been saving from when my children were in college.

Item: Aunt Bess's baby teeth. She couldn't take them with her; neither will I.

Resolve: Take one last fond look at children's baby teeth and contact dentist to see if they are recyclable.

Item: Locks of hair.

I tried to match these up with pictures of people, but there were too many boxes of old photos of people I am not sure were even related. Somebody must have had blond braids, or brown curls.

Resolve: Send my own collection of locks of hair to children in next letter. Put their names on them so they think it was from their first haircut.

Item: Maternal grandmother's blood donor cards from World War II and beyond.

Resolve: Send my blood donor gallon souvenirs to my children in large CARE package. They have been waiting for years to find out how much their mother has given.

Item: Old baby clothes from old baby. The high button shoes and quilted bibs tell me that these were probably not my first apparel.

Resolve: Save old baby clothes for historic value. Send children their bags of treasured baby clothes, including son's bunny suit.

Item: Campaign buttons and postcards, doilies.

Resolve: No point in getting rid of something which might be fun for yet unborn grandchildren to enjoy. Store in drawer where children's artwork is, and send some of that to them with next package of cookies.

Item: Tin boxes filled with pencils, tape and four three-cent stamps.

Resolve: Put in cupboard. Never know when tin box or pencils might come in handy. Buy four 22-cent stamps and use them before the rates go up again.

Item: My baby pictures.

Resolve: How many baby pictures does one need? Can't answer that question. Put in storage.

Item: Old dolls, old books, old flags, old stuff.

Resolve: Should send to the children, but will they appreciate these until they are more mature and have a better grade of clutter of their own? Better save on the shelf with baby pictures.

Item: Suitcases.

Resolve: Lucky find. Can put some of this stuff in them and shove in back of closet or back in storage shed.

See, I'm done and there was nothing to it. I've licked clutter once and for all. The future is bright for my children, and they'll love the surprises already in the mail.

Frogs, Freezes and Funny Dust

Take it from one who knows. If you have recently moved to Florida and have questions about strange and wondrous natural phenomena, go ahead and ask the experts. Just don't identify yourself.

Ten years ago, when we moved here from Up North, I was sure my discovery of the hole-digging frog, frozen orange trees and fluorescent green dust would qualify me for an interview with *National Geographic* or *Southern Living*.

So sure, I revealed who I was on my first call. It was to a local developer's environmental lab. If anyone could tell me the species of frog that had created my swiss cheese lawn, it would be these experts.

I described in detail one September morning how I had discovered the holes and initially blamed the children for punching broomsticks all around our yard. Considering their age at the time, it didn't seem really logical to accuse them, but it was a starting point.

My sleuthing began with my children's denials.

"Why would we go outside and exert ourselves?" they said. "It's too hot and it's too muggy."

That was an alibi I believed. They hadn't left the house since June 28 when we moved from cooler climes.

As I was hanging out laundry, I spotted the next defendant — a large, brown frog sitting in one of the holes.

"Ah-ha," I said. "I'm going to get your name and report you."

So I called the environmental lab.

There was silence on the other end after I finished my tale and asked for the Latin name for the digging frog.

"Armadillo," said the scientific voice. "The armadillo digs. The frog was just sitting in its hole."

How was I to know? We didn't even have frogs in my former Central New York city.

When I called about the green powder coating my car, I disguised my voice and changed my name. "Hi, there," I said, a bit too casually. "Did you know we had a close brush with the moon last night? Everything is covered with bright green powder. Would you like some to analyze it for the space program? My name is Wanda Goatke."

"Goatke? Didn't you call about frogs last month? . . . No? . . . Well, take your car through a car wash today and hose off the pine pollen, Mrs. Goatke."

My third call a year later was about the anteater the cat had been stalking through the back yard. It had a long snout, long tail and somewhat hairy legs.

"Wild boar," said the familiar voice. "What did you say your name is?"

"I just arrived from Chicago. My twin sister lives here. Her voice sounds a lot like mine," I said.

At least I was getting the mysteries solved, even if it took some personal risk. And as an enthusiastic newcomer, I was willing to take other risks to be a good neighbor and do my civic duty.

The first really cold day we had that year, the temperature actually dropped below freezing. Frost on the windshield. Frost on the bananas. Drops of ice on my tomatoes.

As I took my children to school, past the garden center, I became even more alarmed. Someone had left the sprinklers on all night. They were still spraying the garden stock, which was thoroughly coated with ice. It would be a pink slip for some hapless employee, I thought, and economic ruin for the nursery.

I stopped at a pay phone and made my call — a neighborly tip.

"Did you know your sprinklers are coating your lovely orange trees with ice?" I asked, ready to give them my name and address for a thank-you note.

"Yes, we know. That's what we do in Florida to protect our plants in a freeze," they said.

"That's exactly what I thought. I was just having a discussion with my children and they insisted it might be harming the plants, but I said the nursery knows what it is doing," said I.

"My name? . . . Wendy Carrotkey."

Since our junk mail provides us with endless variations on the theme of Grotke, I am well prepared for asking future environmental questions about my adopted land.

I was wondering about an odd-looking plant next to the shed . . .

Domestic Turf Wars

After seven years of camping out, Fluffy has been allowed inside.

Outdoor living was not her idea. It was prompted by severe allergies plaguing the Youngest Child.

On the day of banishment, Middle Child, who had rescued this feline pet nearly 13 years earlier from the pound, was heartbroken. Fluffy had shared her pillow, her toys and her secrets from the first day as her cat.

So she continued to hope that one day the rules would once again change and Fluffy would be allowed to return to her favorite abode. Middle Child, on visits home from college, would sneak her cat in for morsels and cuddles. And she berated me for maintaining The Cat Ban after Youngest Child left home two years ago. She said that once the allergee had moved away, there was no good reason to keep the allergen out.

"I'm not entirely against indoor animals," I said.

"There is still a dog inside," I noted. "He knows his place, which is on the floor, not on my pillow.

"I let Fluffy in for ceremonial occasions such as hurricanes and her birthday. Besides, she has the outdoor companionship of Nicki the Stray," I said to Middle Child.

I told this so-called cat lover that I would be happy to box up The Fluff and take her on a 40-minute ride from home to the airport for a brief and painless flight to Boston where she could be met by this art student who now lives in an apartment which allows pets.

Her faint words over the telephone lines separating us were, "I'm getting a kitten. Fluffy is too old to adjust to snow and city streets, and besides, she has Nicki the Stray for companionship."

We had reached a dramatic stalemate in our mother/daughter relationship. It would take the wisdom of Solomon to decide who should have Fluffy, and who loves her more.

The dramatic change in Fluffy's lifestyle has come from the realization that Nicki has strayed once again, apparently for good. She has been missing for a week. And Fluffy's pitiful, elderly cat greetings from the front door, back door and every window we pass won her the vocal support of Man in My Life who likes cats, even in the house.

So the cat lobby won, and we decided to see how Fluffy would adjust after all these years of having her entry blocked by cat bouncers.

I opened the door wide, expecting her to dash in and slide across the kitchen floor as she used to do. But she sat and stared.

"Here Fluffy, good kitty, come *in* and have your supper," I called last night.

She wouldn't. She gave me a mistrustful yawn and a silent "meow." She swished her tail and stared at me by the back door as if I had lost my mind and might suddenly find it just as she dared to cross the threshold.

"Nice puss. Pretty cat. I have kitty treats and flea powder for you just around the doorway."

Fluffy froze in disbelief.

"We'll call Abbie in New Bedford and you can talk to her about it," I said.

That was evidently good enough. She stretched and walked on little cat feet into the kitchen and looked at her friends the Dog Boys.

I could tell she felt lost in space. There was furniture she had never met and the rest had been rearranged. She thought she was in the Twilight Zone when she settled down on a recliner chair foot rest and found her new sleeping spot none too stable. It was not the house she remembered.

What she remembered was beds and pillows. Now in Abbie's absence she fought me for mine all night. Her fur was in my face every time I rolled over. Her paws kneaded my shoulder. I put her on the floor, but she returned in minutes.

It was not how I had envisioned welcoming her home — waking up every hour to find her on my bedside table, her eyes as bright as the digital clock as she waited to make her next pillow move.

I made *my* move first thing in the morning. The cat went back outside.

If anyone mentions her return to my domain, I think I'll feel a sneeze coming on.

Reeling in the Fish Stories

I won, I won. I won my first fishing contest.

My prize was a $10 bill offered to the first person on our shark fishing expedition to catch something other than catfish.

I could have been rewarded for my catfishing triumph too. I hooked about 16 or maybe 50 of them in a matter of minutes while the others pretended it didn't matter that their lines were fouled in the harbor's artificial reef.

The only shark we saw in five hours was on the fish finder, a colorful video display of blips beneath the black water's surface. However we tempted them, the big blips were not biting. But the little silver ones on the screen dotting the bottom where my line landed were.

And I was happy to be reeling in anything as long as I was on a chartered fishing boat in the middle of the night. Dozens of inedible catfish were just fine.

I like eating shark, though; especially if Man in My Life grills it with barbecue sauce. We had envisioned quite a cookout from our fancied catch.

Instead, I was supplying the chum and bait to the rest of the expedition thanks to my lucky catfish pole.

Lest you think that I am an expert fisherperson, it is not the case. As a Mature Adult, I will bait my hook as long as the bait is not alive.

I am able to cast my line about three feet, and know the difference between catching a reef and a catfish. Sometimes.

I don't really want to hear what the captain is saying about what lives on the bottom and makes those very big blips on his screen. There are some secrets Neptune should keep in the family.

And I wasn't too unhappy that we didn't land a shark, cookout aside.

I remember reading *Moby Dick,* and *The Old Man and the Sea,* and I know how mean something that is big and swims can be.

For that reason I did not see *Jaws* when it came out some years ago. At that time my boy was about 10. We lived in Auburn, N.Y. where the most vicious aquatic creature was a rainbow trout.

My son persuaded his father to take him to see *Jaws.* (Let me say it was about a year before our divorce.) I said in my most sensible maternal voice that something that frightening might give them both nightmares, and frankly I didn't want to have my sleep disturbed in the process. My cautionary advice to the foolhardy pair to come home from the show if it got scary fell on deaf ears.

They wanted to hear the "boombaboombaboomba" theme song and scream themselves silly, but at the same time impress me with how well they could handle the celluloid terror.

And calm they were upon returning home. They were both under control. Not a bit scared. "Just a movie," they said at 11:15 p.m.

But that's not what they said at 3:16 a.m. My son came to *my* side of the bed to talk across me.

"Dad."

"Whayawan?"

"The shark. It's in my room."

"I'll bet you are just dreaming about the scene in which the bloody arm came floating on the beach," said Dad. "I've been dreaming about it too."

"Yes, and remember when . . ."

On and on it went, scene after scene, as the discussion encompassed every detail of the shark attack. I was forced to listen — trapped between them.

"Dad, I'm really scared now," said my 75-pound sixth-grader. "Can I get in bed with you and Mom?"

I knew immediately how canned sardines feel.

"I told you so," I mumbled as the three of us, wide awake, stared at the ceiling until daybreak.

I made a note to mention this episode in divorce court.

I did not dream of sharks after we returned at 1 a.m. from our fishing trip. I was too tired even to take home my whiting, for which I won the non-catfish prize.

But I do want to tell you about the big something which took my bait, hook and sinker. I didn't get a good look in the dark, but I know it wasn't the reef. It was a blip the size of a shark. Honest.

Puss in Boots, or Maybe a Skirt

As a Mature Adult, I should know better, so don't let this get out too far. For the first time in my entire life, after arguing for years with two daughters about the same issue, I have an urge to dress kittens.

I can envision our kittens in little outfits, perhaps some of the baby clothes which I have not yet entrusted to the children as post-graduation presents.

When I had my annual physical, perhaps I should have asked my physician if the desire to dress kittens is because of middle-age hormonal changes, or the empty-nest syndrome, or merely the presence of young kittens in a house populated by elderly pets.

Although Man in My Life said we would have no new animals to add to our aged menagerie of two old dogs and an old cat, he was the one responsible for bringing the two stray kittens inside nearly a month ago.

They were born under some construction debris in the back yard to a nice cat, who has also made herself quite at home — outside.

Mother and twins were separated at about four weeks when she showed signs of poor parenting.

So the babies moved inside, where we could ensure their thriving.

The secret urge to dress them didn't happen immediately. I was satisfied with feeding them milk with little doll bottles.

But they wanted the meaty stuff in the pan instead. So much for my efforts to be a substitute mother.

When I remembered how Youngest Child used to dress her kitten in little blue-checked gowns and bonnets, I cringed for sharply having told her to stop.

In retrospect, she had the right attitude.

The 1976 feline fashion show occurred in Auburn, not Paris. I was recovering on the couch from the flu while Youngest Child was supposed to be resting upstairs. The first well-dressed puss dashed through the living room, soon followed by the second.

"Stop dressing the cats," I shouted.

"Why?" the pre-schooler asked.

I had no answer. I just figured there must be a reason. Mothers don't have to give reasons. They assume them.

All these years her question has haunted me. And now I know the answer should be: "Why not, indeed?"

Mind you, I haven't tried it yet. Tippy would trip over her skirt while she scaled Mount Recliner. And Lo & Behold, named by MML, might have difficulty leaping from table to table in order to knock magazines and coasters everywhere without a split skirt or suitable jogging suit.

The Kittens are adeptly practicing their hunting skills each day on couch pillows, a wooden antelope on the window ledge, and each other.

They have not missed their mother, nor she them, since the day they moved inside. That is fine. I wanted them to love me, and they do. When they were outside, I was the big stranger who promised them catnip when they grew up if only they would come out of their hiding place under the bathtub.

Now, they race when I call them for food and purr when I pet them.

We have little talks about what the well dressed teen-age cat might wear in the next few months. I'm hoping outfitting them will not be as traumatic as trying to pick the right style for Youngest Child when she was in junior high.

If necessary, I will do for them what I did for her: cut out designer labels and sew them on discount store jeans. I also made her wait until the second week of school before buying her fall wardrobe so that we could be sure of what all the other kids were wearing.

I learned that lesson the hard way.

I wonder if The Kittens will trade clothes with their friends. Nothing in Youngest Child's closet was recognizable as something purchased by me, except for the things neither she nor her friends would wear. They were piled in a far corner under ice skates.

MML doesn't know of my plans, so I don't know how he stands on twin-kitten dressing. It wasn't a topic of prenuptial discussions. He said no more pets.

One of these days, when the moon is full and the urge is overwhelming . . .

I'll find out.

The Hole Truth

It was the dogs' dream come true. A hole of immense propor-
tions in their back yard. The hole of holes.

No wonder they threw a day-long fit when the swimming pool
workers came back to complete the project after an unexpected five-
week delay.

The Dog Boys had not seen the original construction in early
March because we had not yet moved into the new house.

Then, the day the hole was dug and initial reinforcement work
started, the project was halted because of an unusual zoning
technicality — namely, that, at least on paper, we had two front
yards, one in the front and one in the back.

A complicated situation, to say the least. It was brought on by
the way our section was platted, and the fact that a non-existent
"road" ran behind what we considered our back yard.

Some people might be overjoyed *not* to have a back yard. They
might like having two front yards.

There is so much work involved with a back yard — extra
mowing over the septic tank, for example. Clotheslines. Vegetable
gardens. Lots of extra chores in back yards that you don't see in
your typical front yard, where you might only have a few hibiscus
to prune.

But back yards are usually where the pool fits, if you plan to
have one. So having two front yards left us with no place to put it,
at least not without a zoning variance.

For us, all's well that ends well, but the Dog Boys did not
understand the situation, hence they initiated a fierce war on
pool workers.

All the dogs saw in the back when they moved into their new
home was the hole of holes, and adjacent mounds of sand which, as
one member of the Board of Zoning Appeals put it, looked like
a moonscape.

If that was what outer space was like, the dogs were ready to
suit up. They thought it was wonderful.

In retrospect, I can understand what was happening in the
canine mind.

The more they looked lovingly at Le Grand Hole, the more they began to think of it as their own. No one had come back to claim it in their first month in the house. By squatters' rights, it was theirs.

They may have even done some neighborhood bragging — convincing Mr. Buttons, a poodle-sort up the street, that in fact they had done the excavation themselves.

By the time the pool workers returned to the job, with the stop-work order removed, the dogs had a proprietary interest as deep as the hole itself.

And the hole was six feet deep at one end. Think of all the bones that could be entombed!

The only other time my dog was privy to something similar was in an excavation of his own doing.

He was younger then, and bored. He was chained outside during the day, during the time his children were in school.

His boredom in the house led to some creative destructive episodes with the couch and toys, which lead to his banishment to the outdoors.

To provide for his creature comfort, I had a carpenter build him a nice doghouse. I placed a large bucket of water near it in the shade. I left him treats.

Everyday, as soon as I was out of his sight, he tipped over the water bucket, tangled himself around twigs and pine cones, barked a lot, and refused to sit in his little house, even when it rained.

I made a wall around his water bucket at 7:30 a.m. He took down the wall at 7:33 a.m., tipped over the bucket at 7:34 a.m. and barked and whined until 3:15 p.m., when the children would find him tangled in bushes and very thirsty.

He deliberately looked neglected and abandoned just to embarrass me in front of my neighbors.

Then he began his dig. I figured it had something to do with the fact that a large nursing home was under construction in the next block. He could see the work from his doghouse's back yard.

They dug. The dog dug. They dug more and moved dirt. The dog dug more.

My daily routine began to include trying to find the sand which he had removed, in order to refill the hole. At first it was the size of a dining room table, then a Ping-Pong table, and as deep as a child's wading pool.

I worried that we would be in trouble with the city for not getting a permit for his project. And now that I am even more educated about such matters, I wonder if it might not have been too close to his rear setback.

The dog finally won. I gave him a bath, had his toenails trimmed, sold the doghouse and moved him back inside. I spent a weekend trying to level that section of the yard again.

He has not won with his new hole. Its earthen interior has been sprayed with concrete, much to his dismay, and the sand hills will be gone by the end of the week.

He's gotten too lazy to dig a new one of his own, which is just as well, because I don't think any future holes are covered under this permit and variance.

Put Away Scales for Christmas

In order to make room for all the Christmas decorations I want to put out this year, I tried to think of things that could be temporarily packed away. My bathroom scales jumped to mind immediately.

That was a fortunate decision because we've been into our annual cookie baking. And no good cook would ever prepare something for company without frequent sampling.

So far the score is: cookies for friends, none, and for "the rest of us," 50 apiece. We've managed to eat everything on our plate and then some.

For the record, "rest of us" includes Man in My Life, his niece, who is visiting from college, and the Dog Boys. I also include myself in that gang of cookie monsters.

It's not easy fixing these treats in Florida. Christmas cookies are best baked at temperatures below 80 degrees. And since we don't experience that weather phenomenon much, other than at 4:30 a.m., some of us have difficulty working with sticky dough.

As usual, I was up to the challenge and vowed that no matter what the final aesthetics, not a crumb would be wasted.

This philosophy has come in handy, except that it has produced this corollary as well: When cookies are involved, waste not, want more. In other words, you can't eat just one.

Usually my holiday baking has taken a traditional form. I make the dough, sample it, refrigerate the remainder, roll out and stamp out shapes with my cookie cutters.

However, I had a rare opportunity this year to try something new and special. And I knew it would be a wonderful surprise for Man in My Life in the weeks before we are to wed.

As a gesture of her prenuptial acceptance of me, the groom's aunt gave me a large clay cookie mold in the shape of a sheep.

What could be a more fitting way to start the cookie season than to make a gingerbread sheep cookie for my intended? It could become a new tradition.

To my way of thinking, cooking should never be so complicated that one must always read directions. My grandmother always added a "pinch of this" and a "dash of that," and her cakes and cookies could have won prizes in the Ohio State Fair.

Following her style, I bypassed step one with the sheep cookie mold (namely reading how to use it), and lathered it with the dark gingerbread paste. I figure the mix was designed for people who live Up North, rather than those of us who bake in our bathing suits.

How shall I put this? The pottery should have been treated with Teflon or motor oil. I had a bit of unexpected difficulty extracting the sheep cookie from its mold and had to spend time reshaping the basic design, free-form.

When the cookies came out of the oven, I proudly took it to Man in My Life. He was busy baking to perfection his mother's infallible oatmeal cookies. They were perfect as usual. And, his niece was finishing her third batch of sugar cookies, all neatly trimmed with red and green sparkles.

"I baked this for you," I said to MML.

Very tactfully he said, "It looks like road kill."

"Wait until I put the frosting on so you can see its eyes and tail," I said. "And I will add a heart, so you know it is from me.

"It just isn't finished yet," I added.

"I saw something like that in the side yard yesterday," said his niece with the twinkling cookie stars.

"If I write 'I love you' on it in green frosting, it is yours forever," I said.

114

I knew they were making fun of my cookie because they were jealous. They wished they had thought of it. They want to be able to brag to my children when they come home for the holidays that the sheep cookie is theirs — and that it is just too good to eat. Something to frame. The art guild will beg to hang it in its new center.

No, I will not let their attitude trouble me or take away my holiday spirit.

Instead, I will set a good example, and be polite and accept samples of oatmeal, peanut butter and sugar cookies, no matter what the color or shape.

We won't need to worry about what anybody else, friends or family thinks about our baking projects. The cookies will be long gone, and the bathroom scales will return, covered with red and green bows.

I don't know why I didn't think of making them a central part of the holiday decorations in the first place.

Bunny Suits
and Other Heirlooms

It came as a shock this weekend that my son was not waiting for the day that I would recognize his maturity and present him with his bunny suit.

Not only had he thoughtlessly forgotten about the tiny, zippered white coverall which he outgrew the first week of his life in 1964, but he was careful not to urge me to rush to the post office with it.

I confess that I have saved a few special things from my children's early years. Since these treasures have survived at least two moves, including the big one to Florida years ago, their value has increased like vintage wine.

Besides the terry cloth bunny suit, which no longer sports its puffy tail, I'm sure my closet holds a sack of other infant clothes that he wore, such as the tiny red- and white-striped flannel pajamas that a friend made for the baby shower.

Unfortunately, my boy was nine pounds at birth and born in the summer. As an inexperienced new mother, I wanted to make sure Christopher was warm enough. I also wanted him to be healthy in Buffalo's fresh air (an oxymoron). So I took him out in the July sunshine wrapped well.

"I don't think he needs his snowsuit, it's 87 degrees," intervened his paternal grandmother.

Probably the flannel pajamas would have been too much as well. I reluctantly and fearfully took him down to his undershirt and diapers for his outing in the carriage. He survived my maternal cautiousness.

"But why are you keeping his bunny suit?" Man in My Life asked recently, as he surveyed what, in his view, was the clutter surrounding me.

"Christopher will want this some day. He will want to have it framed or stuffed to show his children that he has not always been 6-feet, 4-inches tall," I said.

"And I have other special souvenirs of my children's childhood," I said rashly, risking an immediate end to the new

116

dating relationship.

"They will be so pleased when I send them locks of their hair, first teeth harvested by the Tooth Fairy, art and stories from first grade, their favorite childhood books and decorations they made each year for the Christmas tree. I just wish I had done a better job of labeling whose is which," I said. "But I have it all in a rather uncentralized system of storage, called 'available drawers and boxes.' I know they will be thrilled."

My friend's look was doubtful.

"Let's call Christopher. We'll see who's right," I said Sunday morning. "Don't you think I know my child?"

"Hello," I said to the sleepy voice on the other end. "I was wondering how you feel about your bunny suit."

"Who did you say was calling?" said the alarmed voice in Washington.

"Just tell the man I am putting on the line how much you are looking forward to one day receiving the bunny suit and the rest of your special childhood treasures," I said, "and remember your inheritance as you answer objectively."

I handed the phone to MML. Silence and smiles in Florida as Washington talked.

Florida handed the phone back to me.

"So, what did you tell him?" I asked my son.

"Man talk," said Washington. "But don't feel you need to use overnight mail to send me the bunny suit."

I hung up. "You see, Christopher does want it, but just not right now," I said.

There was a sigh from the person sitting across from me.

"Would you like to see what I'm saving for his sisters? I have Abbie's first scribble and Jenny's bib and a home-made Teddy bear. It looks more like a rabbit. She would have taken it to college but she didn't have room at the last minute."

"I've seen enough. Actually, I've seen too much," said he.

I don't think my son was persuasive enough. I don't think he is sufficiently mature to receive the bunny suit just yet. Maybe on his birthday in July, I'll send it along with his baby blankets and summer snowsuit.

Darwin's Theory of Agriculture

Woodsman, spare that tree.

He knows that taking it, along with two other spindly ones, will help the survivors in the pine grove improve their looks and life.

Do you think his arguments impress me? No. I want them all saved, no matter what.

We are having some yardwork done prior to our move — some general pruning and trimming. The woodsman, who knows his stuff, has made a compelling case for removing these three scrawny trees. However, he has lost.

I figure it is not up to me to decide which trees should live and which should die. I cannot be a part of pulling their plugs, so to speak.

Woodsman rolls his eyes back, and appeals to my husband. I start unwinding the dog's chain and wrapping it around my waist.

"The big trees will grow better," says Man in My Life, a scientist.

"Aren't the little trees pretty? See how green they look against the blue sky?" I say to Woodsman and MML.

In my heart I know they are right, but they are dealing with someone who could not bear to thin the radishes she planted from seed.

It was a choice that was too difficult. How could I now wrench handfuls of sprouts from my rows, just so one or two plants would have room to grow? I talked to them instead.

"Hi guys. It's up to you. Battle it out," I said to my plants.

"You can't expect the farmer to figure this stuff out for you. If it gets too crowded, some of you just trail over to the next row. There is more room among the onions."

I didn't have much success reasoning with the radishes. But that was their problem. My hands were clean.

One year Up North, when the children were very young, I planted a small garden in a plot of land about the size of a picnic table.

Oldest Child, then about three, wanted to help.

I knew just how helpful he would be, walking through my neatly tilled rows and sitting on the squash.

So I gave him a reasonable option.

"How would you like to have your own little garden?" I asked.

"Mommy will give you all her extra seeds and beans and plants. All you have to do is watch her and then plant your garden.

"Then every few days, water your plants and weed them. Won't this be fun?" I asked.

He thought so. And we took up city farming together.

As I knew would happen, the novelty wore off, and Oldest Child rarely returned to water and weed. I did not interfere. His garden was his responsibility. When The Harvest came, he would learn what he should have done.

I watered and weeded, and thinned my radishes.

The Harvest came. It was *his*.

My crops failed, for reasons that baffle me. None of the radishes I selected for success chose to accept the challenge. The ones I pulled out and handed to my boy, produced red, tart salad fixings.

He also had an ear or two of corn. He had tomatoes. He had lettuce and carrots among his thicket of weeds.

The sun must have been too strong on my "field." Maybe I gave my plants a quart or so too much water. Maybe I should have rented a mule and done some plowing. Maybe I shouldn't have thinned my plants or bothered with the weeding. Perhaps there is a symbiotic relationship between radishes and certain members of the weed family.

I have never had the same ambition in the vegetable patch since that fateful summer.

And it made me question my ability to determine what should die in my yard so others might live.

I mentioned this ethical dilemma to a co-worker. She responded by telling me about her 5-year-old son's science project. He was learning about experiments and had come up with a question of his own to solve scientifically: "Will my potato grow in a closet?"

The answer is "yes."

Potatoes will grow nicely in a closet or pantry or refrigerator, but not in my garden. I could have told him that. So maybe I have had the wrong approach. I learned from one kindergartner to let the garden grow at will. And now another has taught me that it can be successfully planted in a closet. I don't know what the rules are for weeding and thinning under such novel conditions, however.

Woodsman, while you're at it, spare that potato.

Recycling Goes to the Dogs

As serendipity would have it, I have stumbled on the solution to our county's recycling dilemma.

Our politicians and their subcommittees have spent untold hours in deliberation with no resolution in sight.

They don't know whether to set up a program of recycling by which homeowners would separate various items before placing them at the curb for collection, or by letting someone do the sorting for them at the dump.

While I feel confident that I can tell the difference between an aluminum can and a newspaper and can separate them myself, apparently there is a concern by our leaders that others might not have been blessed with such discernment and may need or want someone to do it for them.

And if they press on for what is called a tail-end system, where all trash and garbage is taken to one central site for people to sort among the aggregate muck, there may be some foolish outcry about health hazards and working conditions and the like. I'm convinced that my solution may just save the day.

Dog power. That's it. Don't laugh. Dog power. My idea came to me the other day when I arrived home from work to a house which looked liked it had been hit by an earthquake.

Sometime between lunch, when I put the dogs out briefly, and 5 p.m., when I returned, someone (and I'm not naming names) dove into the garbage and sorted its contents into three rooms.

Someone took a cluster of tin cans (formerly containing pet food) into his nest between the drapes and the coffee table.

Someone took wet garbage, mostly coffee grounds, into the center of the living room. Someone took paper products, best described as the remnants of Chinese food take-out cartons, and shredded them under the dining room table.

In the center of the kitchen floor, neatly separated from other recyclables, was a rubber band, string and a piece of plastic.

Someone did not look a bit remorseful.

Now, if Someone, who is deaf, canine and old can tell the difference and in such short order separate and classify such items, *without* training, think what would happen *with* on-the-job instruction?

And that's just one dog. And he isn't even mine. He belongs to Man in My Life. My dog already knows the difference between cat food and dog food, dirty clothes and his toys. As a young fellow, he could pick the expensive new doll from the toy box and chew just it.

He has potential as well.

And I'm sure, that if a call went out to the public, there would be many canine volunteers from homes across this land.

And there might even be specialists sent in from other states. This summer, I met a dog named Jake, who lives with an otherwise nice family Up North.

Jake, a very large mix of mastiff, Great Dane and bulldog, is an expert in cloth. At all times he must have something cloth in his mouth. That something may be his owner's boxer shorts (from the laundry), a folded sheet (from the linen closet) or the table cloth (from the table).

While his general canine behavior is not winning him awards in obedience school (he bit the trainer and earned only an attendance certificate), Jake's potential may be undeveloped as a recycler.

His owners will be very happy at a chance to get rid of him for a worthy cause. And if Jake and other dogs are doing what they like to do best, their entire attitude about life and themselves may improve.

Dog labor is cheap, unless some animal activists start making demands. I have seen dogs tip over garbage cans and begin sorting just for the treats found therein. No other pay is needed.

Though I've been too busy lately to work out all the details, I think it is an idea which has merit.

And maybe we will even get some national recognition for our advanced concept of recycling.

I and my team of experts will be available for another demonstration as soon as I get this first one cleaned up.

Forecast on Fleas

Maybe there truly is a connection between the weather and this year's superior hatch of fleas.

I can't remember if fleas are worse when it has been dry, wet, hot or cold, although I have heard that some combination of these conditions creates the bumper crop which is now terrorizing our hapless animals.

A possible clue was on the radio station's morning weather report. It followed the national news, to which we half-listen on the clock radio.

The local announcer came on with these weather tidbits. He forecast that we would have "more of the same" that day — a mixture of sun and rain.

Then he added, "Currently, it is 79 degrees . . . and dark."

It woke me right up. A darkness report on the weather.

That was the most helpful piece of information that we had at that hour in a long time. Could we expect brightness reports later on, peaking at noon?

I immediately knew what to expect when I opened my eyes. Dark. And just how hot that darkness was. Seventy-nine degrees worth.

Now, if he had only mentioned how much worse we could expect the fleas under such conditions.

The dogs are dark, making it difficult to find the fleas which have taken over their entire bodies, no matter what we do to eliminate them.

While I am philosophical about the inability to rid dogs and cats of fleas, Man in My Life takes the situation personally.

That is because his dog hosts the county's largest flea market. MML claims that his dog is a magnet for every flea that is looking for a free lunch within a 75-mile radius of our house.

MML keeps hoping, that with all the preparations and frequent baths he gives the Dog Boys and The Kittens, that just once, his efforts will be rewarded and there will be no more fleas. Ever. I think he deserves that.

Yet, within an hour of a bath and dip, his dog is scratching again. MML mumbles things I do not want to hear, about not having any more pets. Ever.

Last week alone, he bathed the dogs on Sunday; had his dog shorn and bathed on Tuesday; washed and sprayed them again Friday, removing hundreds more fleas in the process.

The dogs are used to their bath and dip by this time in their lives. They put up with it without much of a struggle, even though they must be dragged to their wash tub and hoisted unceremoniously into the bubbles.

The Kittens provide a new challenge. I wouldn't have bothered washing them for just a few fleas, but MML is determined to have victory over these pests at all costs.

So he asked me to help him bathe the girls. They were not pleased, and I think I will be much too busy to help when he decides to shampoo them again next weekend. My job was to hold them, while he applied the special soap. I learned that kittens do not naturally hold still when wet. In fact, they become quite slippery.

I fear that since we are having "more of the same" weather for a while, the fleas are likely to plague us until there is a change of seasons sometime in December.

In his flea fight, MML now is adding brewer's yeast and garlic to the pets' food. All it has done so far is make The Kittens and dogs more frisky. Who knows what it is doing to their tenants.

He mutters about the day when the house will be free of furry critters, and he can sell his stock in flea bombs.

I have a better alternative. MML is using a new mouthwash which is so potent it has taken the flowers off the wallpaper in the bathroom when he exhales after rinsing with it.

It is so strong, I believe if enough of our soldiers in the Middle East used it simultaneously and breathed in the direction of Iraq, the enemy troops would flee instantly.

With something this potent, it must have domestic application as well.

My theory is this: if MML would dip the dogs in this mouthwash, it would drive the fleas away — at least as far as the county line.

Otherwise, the situation is dark indeed and I think we can expect more of the same.

Family Recipes for Yuk

A friend recently fixed "HRS" stew for me. It was tasty, but based on looks alone should only be served to adults. Kids immediately dash for the phone and dial the abuse hotline.

It was grey, and had yellow peas, little, round meat things and noodles, not the sort of meal that one would ever set before young or teen-age children. At least in my house.

Despite my best efforts to teach them food tolerance, often by setting a good example, my offspring remained difficult to please.

And suspicious. They were suspicious of everything that could not be spelled with some combination of letters from the word "hamburger."

Even then, the Middle Child was a purist. She wanted her ground beef made by fast-food pressers, and did not want it crumbled into sauce or fashioned into little balls in stew.

She would spend a full five minutes studying her plate before venturing a bite. She chewed slowly, moved and sorted vegetables until everyone left the table and it was safe to give The Dog his due.

Sigh.

Another friend of mine recently told me all her grown children were home for Mother's Day weekend and had looked forward to her cooking.

I stuck my fingers in my ears and said, "La la la la" to drown out her story. I didn't want to hear it. She said she cooked and baked for two weeks in advance — all the kids' favorite recipes. And they all thanked her and praised her and said they missed her dearly.

I could spend two weeks trying to figure out if my children ever had any favorite recipes of dishes that I made. And then we would go out to eat.

Frankly, I don't think that I was a bad cook. I think they were bad eaters. There is a difference. And because I was a mother who did not lay the guilt trips on them as condiments, they did not fear eating peas in purgatory or adding to world starvation if they did not finish their macaroni salad.

I was too nice at the dinner table.

If they said, "Yuk, what is that?" I'd try to tell them that Yuk was good for them, and then pull out a recipe I had just read in a check-out counter magazine for one of 44 ways to delight your family with Yuk. The photos showed rosy-cheeked, scrubbed children wearing pinafores helping their mother stir food and saying, "Yum, we love your Yuk, Mom."

There would be testimonials from three mothers from different regions of the United States. One single working parent said her children begged for more Yuk because it was so nutritious and healthful. He was 5 years old and said it tasted better than his favorite tofu.

My children were unimpressed. "Can we go out to eat? Look, even The Dog won't try this stuff."

Where had I gone wrong? Surely not in menu selection. Lack of guilt? Too much democracy? They had all started off with the same strained baby foods and had eaten heartily. Should I have kept them on pureed carrots until high school graduation?

Now that I think about it, they did like sauces; apple and hot fudge.

They are all doing their own cooking these days, or are eating out all the time. I don't know what they fix to eat, because they haven't called home for any treasured family recipes.

Maybe, after all these years of ingratitude at the table, they are afraid to admit they secretly liked Red Flannel Hash, banana surprise and one-step microwave chicken.

I'll give them a chance to save face. I'll just send them my recipes as little gifts now and then, and I'll include H R S stew, now that they are more mature.

A Fiduciary Balancing Act

I'm trying to decide if I should start off the New Year by resolving to balance my checkbook. But I probably won't. There is just too much involved.

It's not just using the calculator once a month to see if the bank and I agree, I need to locate the calculator first. It was last seen heading toward a pile of Christmas cards on the left corner of the kitchen table.

1987 Christmas cards. But it might not be there at all, and I will end up cleaning a surface of the house that is better left alone.

As a Mature Adult, I have discovered this law: One "good" project sets four or five bad ones in motion.

Beyond finding the calculator, I would need to open a new checking account.

Two years ago when I did that to solve other problems which you do not want to hear about, I promised my bankers that this time things would be different. I would be their model customer. They would be able to feature me in banking advertisements as a true success story — someone who had taken the fiduciary pledge in front of all the tellers at the drive-in window.

I promised solemnly, on penalty of having my ATM card suspended, that I would, each month, open my bank statements, put my checks in order, tally them against all existing records and find a balance in the process.

My resolve lasted until the middle of the month when the fat envelope of cancelled checks arrived.

I had things to do, places to go and people to see that day.

I tucked it in a drawer for a rainy day. The sun has been shining ever since. I waited for a rainy weekend, then a rainy month. I have a drawer full of cancelled checks and a dry umbrella.

That's my problem. I balanced my checkbook when I lived Up North. It either rained or snowed daily, so there was plenty of time to take care of such things as cultivating appropriate banking relationships. I dusted Up North, read long novels during blizzards and cooked homemade soup.

I had the feeling that moving to a sunnier clime would be a corrupting influence on an otherwise responsible mother of three. I feared that my resolve would fade in the bright sunshine, along with my furniture and paintings. I suspected I would become lazy and inclined not to iron in January if the weather were right for a picnic.

It was true. There is no incentive to spend hours trying to decipher my handwriting in my check register. My bank doesn't send prizes to customers who hit all their numbers on the nose.

Now that it has been two full years since my unopened statements were sent, I don't know where to begin.

And does it matter in the cosmic scheme of things anyway? Cancelled checks are just as likely to be swallowed up in a black hole as socks or Scotch tape or anything else.

A friend of mine is not satisfied until he balances his checkbook to the penny. He can't abide a 17-cents differential. I can. I can go as high as 40 — dollars, not cents — depending on circumstances.

He is concerned, because I live with such carefree abandon, that I am secretly critical of those who take their banking responsibilities seriously. Not so. I am a tolerant person.

I just ask the same courtesy of my favorite financial institution.

We have learned to co-exist pretty well through the years. My guess at the balance is pretty good — and I have actually had fewer overdrafts than when I worked hard to keep track of each entry.

On days like today when something, such as the need for a viable New Year's resolution, prompts me to examine areas of delinquency in my life — checkbook guilt, for example — I am tempted to look a little further down the list of opportunities for improvement.

Maybe answering those 1987 Christmas cards.

On Being a Presidential 'Moonie'

The President of the United States said to go outside and look at the moon. So we did.

I wondered as we stood in the middle of the street at 10:15 p.m. August 16, if George Bush had said jump off the bridge, would we have complied as well? It was a question I always asked of my children when they said they had done something because a friend had told them to. I think the same principle was involved here, but I'm reluctant to admit I have given in to peer or presidential pressure.

So there we stood, Man in My Life and I, in the center of the asphalt, looking up at the Southern sky and swatting mosquitoes.

The insect pests were our only companions in moon gazing on our street. Lunar patriotism seemed to be on the wane.

A cat sat on a dumpster, but we saw no one else in the neighborhood in the center of the road for the unobstructed view of the unusual event.

Where was everybody? Inside watching an instant replay on television? Rushing up to the new mall to buy telescopes?

I was impressed with the excellent view of the moon's round shape during the total eclipse. For some reason, forgetting my fourth grade science, I figured that the moon would be in the sky, shining like a silver dollar one minute, then blackened from all view the next.

I was astonished that I could actually see it better and that it gave me a sense of living on a planet. Paying bills, dieting and making wedding plans had limited my perspective of where I fit in with Mars, Venus and Saturn, and other elements of the universe.

MML taught science for a number of years, so as I straddled the street's white line, and hummed songs, such as *Shine on Harvest Moon,* he explained what gave the moon its copper hue, and told me why I wouldn't be able to follow Mr. Bush's suggestion to watch the eclipse if we lived in California because of time changes.

Actually, the lunar eclipse was a satisfying natural event, not like Halley's Comet. I stood out in the road for that one too, holding in one hand a star-gazing map from *The New York Times,* and in the other, binoculars.

I was unable to read the map with binoculars so I had to rely on some fancy guesswork as to the comet's location, which failed. Either I saw the comet along with everything else in the sky that night, or it wasn't really there.

My fourth grade teacher said comets had tails. I believed her. I just didn't see any.

In fact, I trusted her completely when she told us about Pluto and the Milky Way. It came as a great shock a few years ago to attend Middle Child's parent's night at junior high, and observe a science class.

Her teacher gave an abbreviated version of the fall curriculum which focused on astronomy. At first I wondered if I were in the wrong school — if I had wandered into an advanced college course instead?

Then I wondered if I had day-dreamed throughout my entire fourth grade science class. Did my daughter's teacher know Galileo personally to get all this information that was unfamiliar to me?

When I got home the mystery of my mental black hole was solved.

Everything my offspring was learning had been discovered *after* I had gone to school. I was in the lost-in-space generation.

It is comforting to know, however, that the moon hasn't changed much in that time, and that it hasn't been platted for development yet.

I am so happy to oblige the president on these simple requests to look at the moon.

I'd just like him to arrange the next eclipse when the mosquitoes aren't in season. There might be more support from my neighbors and we could get up a chorus to harmonize on the moon songs.

About the Author

Linda Grotke Salisbury, author of *Good-bye Tomato, Hello Florida* and *Read My Lips: No New Pets* is a columnist and writer for the *Sarasota Herald-Tribune*. She grew up on Long Island, and majored in English at Oberlin College. Before moving to Florida in 1978, she wore earmuffs in Buffalo, Chicago and Auburn, New York. Her career in journalism began at the *Auburn Citizen,* then after moving to Charlotte County, she was reporter and later bureau chief for the *Sarasota Herald-Tribune*. She also is a book reviewer for *The Justice Professional*. She is married to Jim Salisbury, and their blended family includes Chris, Abigail and Jen Grotke, Deb Salisbury, The Dog Boys and several tabbies.

Give a Gift that Laughs!

For autographed copies of Linda Grotke Salisbury's

Read My Lips: No New Pets

and

Good-bye Tomato, Hello Florida

and information on other new titles from Tabby House Books
send a check or money order with this coupon to

TABBY HOUSE BOOKS
4429 Shady Lane, Charlotte Harbor, FL 33980

Send me

_____ copies of Read My Lips: No New Pets $8.95 each

_____ copies of Good-bye Tomato, Hello Florida $8.95 each

(I'm adding $2.00 per book for postage and handling and
6% sales tax for Florida residents)

Total Enclosed _____

Please autograph as follows: (Please print)   Circle title

_____   Lips   Tomato
_____   Lips   Tomato
_____   Lips   Tomato
_____   Lips   Tomato

If you purchased your copy elsewhere or received one as a gift, and
would like to have it autographed, please return to Tabby House
Books along with $2 for postage and handling and the name you
would like inscribed.

Send my books to: (Please print)

_____
Name

_____
Street

_____
City   State   Zip